New Mexico Dreamscapes V

Bobby J. Jones

Copyright © 2018 Bobby J. Jones

All rights reserved.

ISBN: 10: 1727555864

ISBN-13: 978-1727555868

DEDICATION

This coloring book with its beautiful images is dedicated to the loving memory of my maternal grandfather Edward Watts Brown (1904-1959).

CONTENTS

Acknowledgment……………………………………………...……………………………………......Page vii
Image 1…………………………………………………………………………………………………..Page 2
Image 2…………………………………………………………………………………………………..Page 4
Image 3…………………………………………………………………………………………………..Page 6
Image 4…………………………………………………………………………………………………..Page 8
Image 5………………………………………………………………………………………………….Page 10
Image 6………………………………………………………………………………………………….Page 12
Image 7………………………………………………………………………………………………….Page 14
Image 8………………………………………………………………………………………………….Page 16
Image 9………………………………………………………………………………………………....Page18
Image 10…..…………………………………………………………………………………………….Page 20
Image 11………………………………………………………………………………………………...Page 22
Image 12……………………………………………………………………………………...…………Page 24
Image 13………………………………………………………………………………………………...Page 26
Image 14………………………………………………………………………………………………...Page 28
Image 15………………………………………………………………………………………………...Page 30
Image 16………………………………………………………………………………………………...Page 32
Image 17………………………………………………………………………………………………...Page 34
Image 18………………………………………………………………………………………………...Page 36
Image 19………………………………………………………………………………………………...Page 38
Image 20………………………………………………………………………………………………...Page 40
Image 21………………………………………………………………………………………………...Page 42
Image 22………………………………………………………………………………………………...Page 44
Image 23…………………………………………………………………………………………….....Page 46
Image 24………………………………………………………………………………………………...Page 48
Image 25………………………………………………………………………………………………...Page 50
Image 26………………………………………………………………………………………………...Page 52
Image 27………………………………………………………………………………………………...Page 54
Image 28……………………………………………………………………………………...…………Page 56
Image 29………………………………………………………………………………………………...Page 58
Image 30………………………………………………………………………………………………...Page 60
Image 31………………………………………………………………………………………………...Page 62
Image 32………………………………………………………………………………………………...Page 64
Image 33………………………………………………………………………………………………...Page 66
Image 34………………………………………………………………………………………………...Page 68
Image 35………………………………………………………………………………………………...Page 70
Image 36………………………………………………………………………………………………...Page 72
Image 37………………………………………………………………………………………………...Page 74
Image 38………………………………………………………………………………………………...Page 76
Image 39………………………………………………………………………………………………...Page 78
Image 40………………………………………………………………………………………………...Page 80
Image 41………………………………………………………………………………………………...Page 82
Image 42………………………………………………………………………………………………...Page 84
Image 43………………………………………………………………………………………………...Page 86
Image 44………………………………………………………………………………………………...Page 88
Image 45………………………………………………………………………………………………...Page 90
Image 46………………………………………………………………………………………………...Page 92
Image 47………………………………………………………………………………………………...Page 94
Image 48………………………………………………………………………………………………...Page 96
Image 49………………………………………………………………………………………………...Page 98

Image 50	Page 100
Image 51	Page 102
Image 52	Page 104
Image 53	Page 106
Image 54	Page 108
Image 55	Page 110
Image 56	Page 112
Image 57	Page 114
Image 58	Page 116
Image 59	Page 118
Image 60	Page 120
Image 61	Page 122
Image 62	Page 124
Image 63	Page 126
Image 64	Page 128
Image 65	Page 130
Image 66	Page 132
Image 67	Page 134
Image 68	Page 136
Image 69	Page 138
About The Author	Page 140

New Mexico Dreamscapes V

New Mexico Dreamscapes V

I acknowledge my maternal grandfather Edward Watts Brown in this coloring book. My grandfather was born in Henrietta, Clay County, Texas on July 10, 1904 to Edward Innis Brown and Mary Adeline Watts Brown. My grandfather was the oldest son out of four sons and three daughters.

Edward Watts Brown was raised in Henrietta, Clay County, Texas and graduated from Henrietta High School in 1922. He attended Texas A&M University and was in The Corps of Cadets at this Texas university.

He was a member of The Class of 1928. During his Junior year, Edward was a member of The Panhandle Club and also a member of Intercollegiate Poultry Judging Team.

This team travelled to Chicago in 1926. There were ten states represented in this poultry judging contest. Texas placed second in production and sixth in the whole contest.

My maternal grandfather majored in Animal Husbandry at Texas A&M. He developed a love for animals as a child while growing up in a small Texas town near The Red River. Edward earned a full four year scholarship at Texas A&M. By his senior year, there were no monetary funds left to complete his last semester of his senior year.

He travelled back home to Lubbock to help support his parents and his family by working for Armour & Swift Company. By this time my, great grandfather moved his family from Henrietta, Clay County, Texas to Lubbock, Lubbock County, Texas. During this time, my grandfather met my grandmother during her senior year at Texas Technological College in 1931.

On March 5, 1932, Edward married Sue Morrison Brown at The Broadway Church of Christ in Lubbock, Lubbock County, Texas. My grandparents lived on 16th Street with my maternal grandmother's family until 1937 when my mother's family moved to Abernathy, Lubbock/Hale Counties, Texas. My great grandparents had a farm in Abernathy. This farm was sold in 1940. The money from this real estate sale helped to buy my great grandparents' house on 28th in

Lubbock, Lubbock County, Texas. My grandparents were able to buy their 110 acre farm west of Lubbock near Reese Air Force Base. The house is currently on Upland Avenue between 19th Street and 4th Street. At the time , my grandparents moved their family into this house.

Their house was a part of the Carlisle community in Lubbock County. This house is where my mom and her sisters spent their childhood. This house was known as Grandma's house in Lubbock. My grandfather was a farmer and grew livestock on this farm until his death on November 15, 1959 from injuries received from a farm accident in Crosby County, Texas .

My grandparents were the parents of three daughters. They were Margaret, Kate and Sue. My grandfather always wanted a son . When he passed away in 1959, he was the grandfather of three grandsons and a granddaughter. I always thought that he would have enjoyed his other grandchildren that were born after his death (two more granddaughters and three more grandsons). I always wanted to know about more my maternal grandfather Edward Watts Brown.

I wish that I could have known my maternal grandfather. The stories that I heard about him as a child focused upon being a grandfather that loved children and animals. He also took the time to teach others how to do things on the farm.

My mom always shared her memories of waking up early in the morning to milk the cows with her daddy before 5 am. He always cooked breakfast in the kitchen every morning. He would sing and bang on the pots and pan while preparing the morning meal. He also encouraged others to achieve a higher education.

My grandmother shared with me before she passed away in 1983. My grandfather was the only man that she ever loved. She was a widow for 23 years.

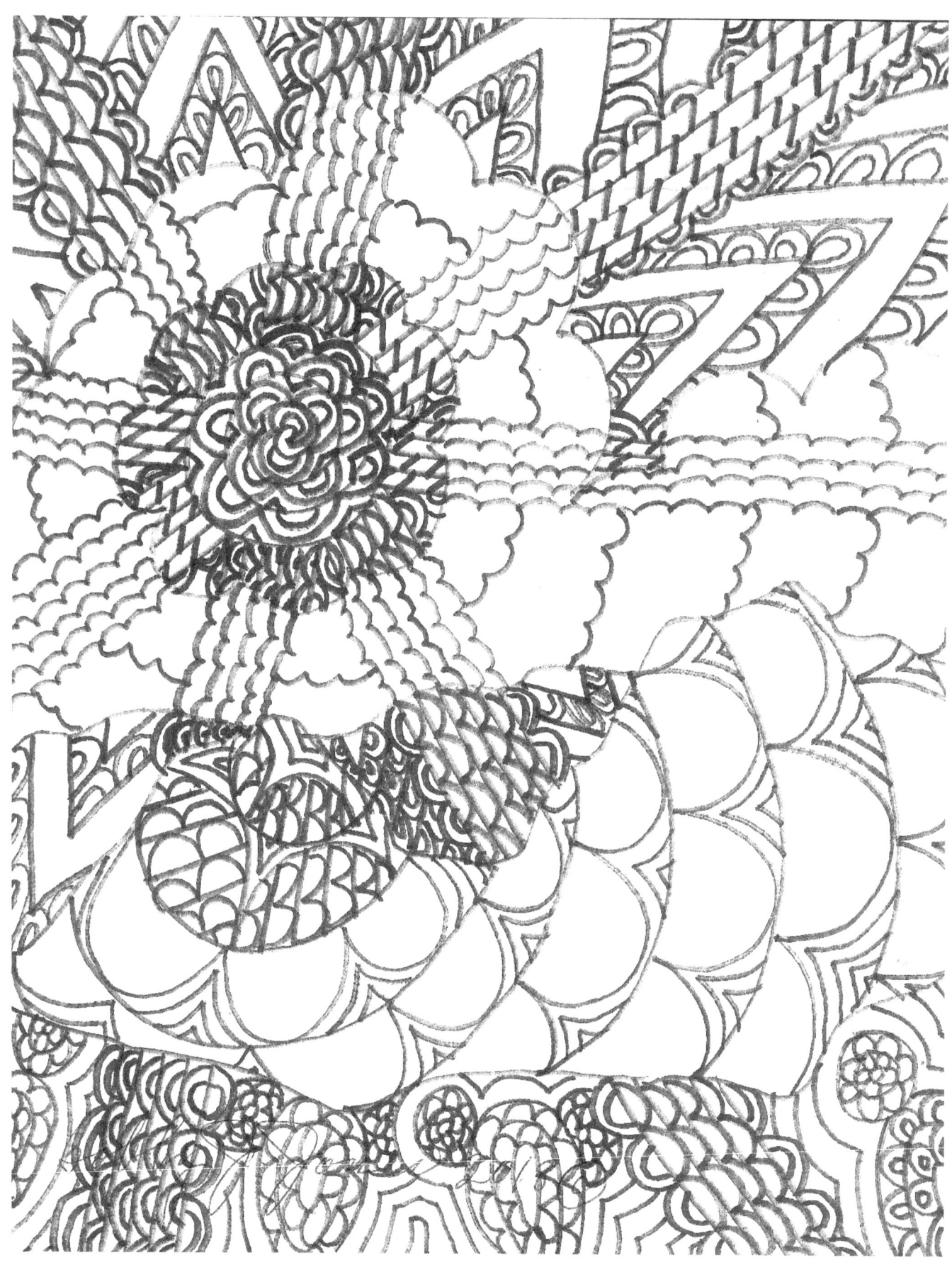

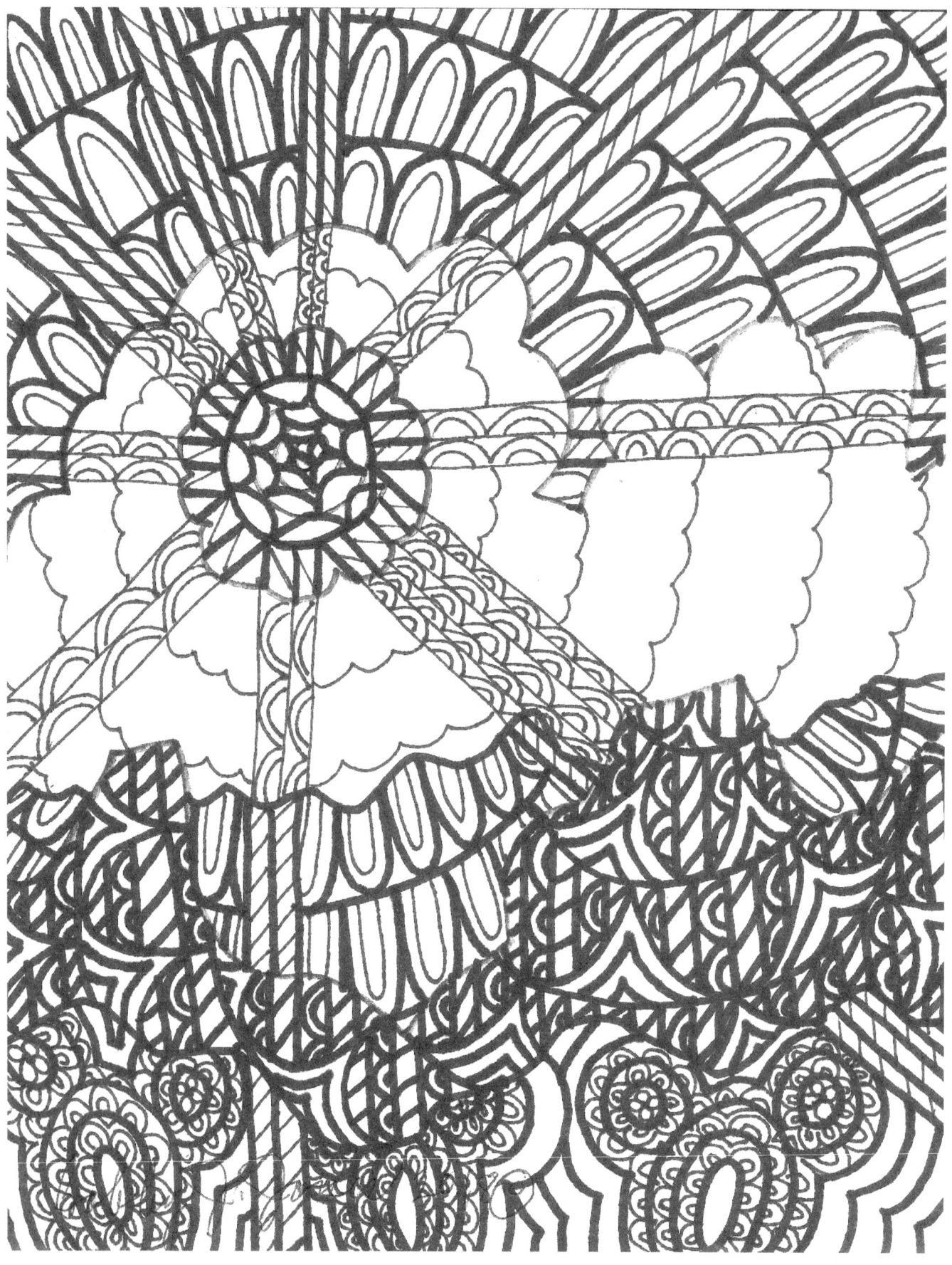

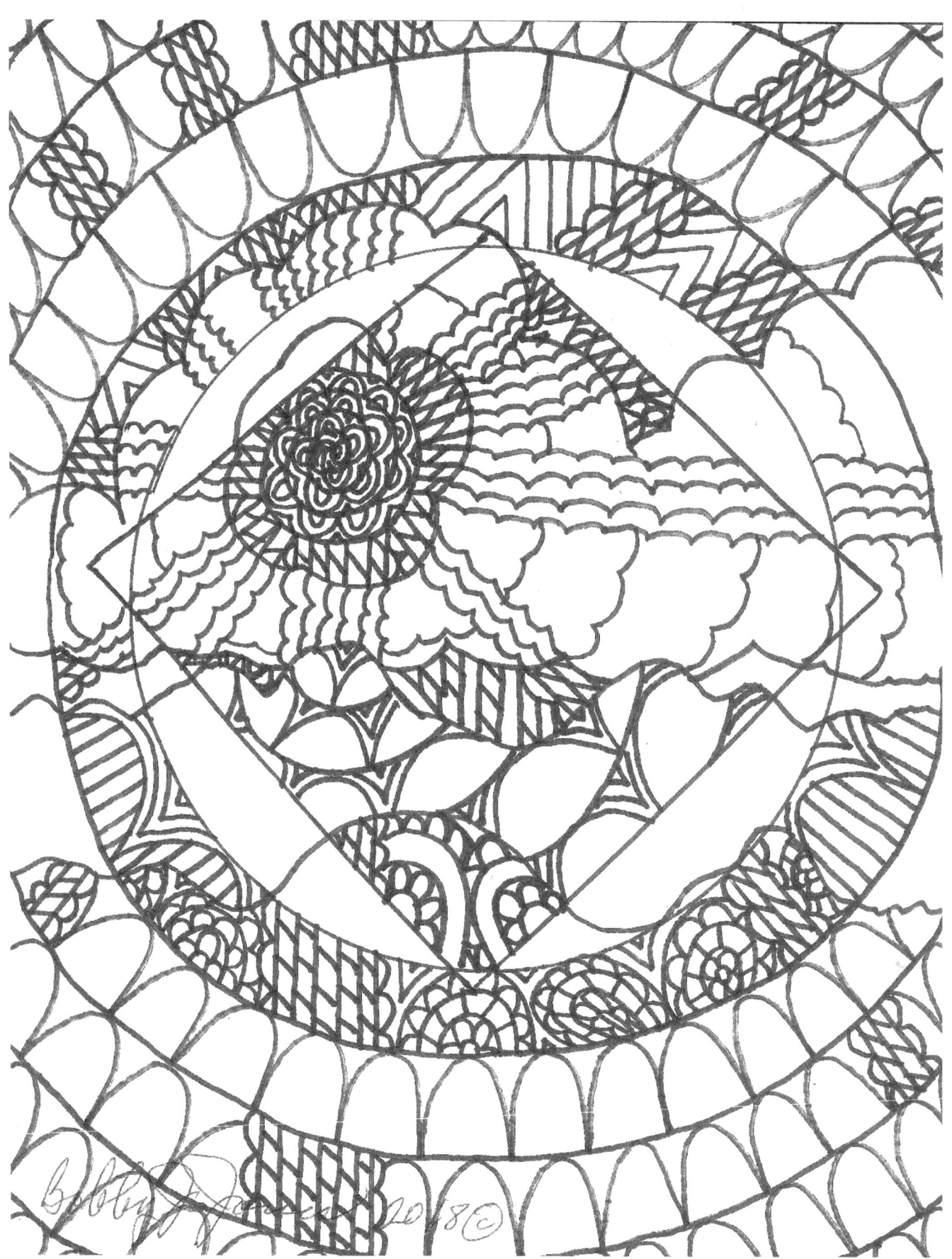

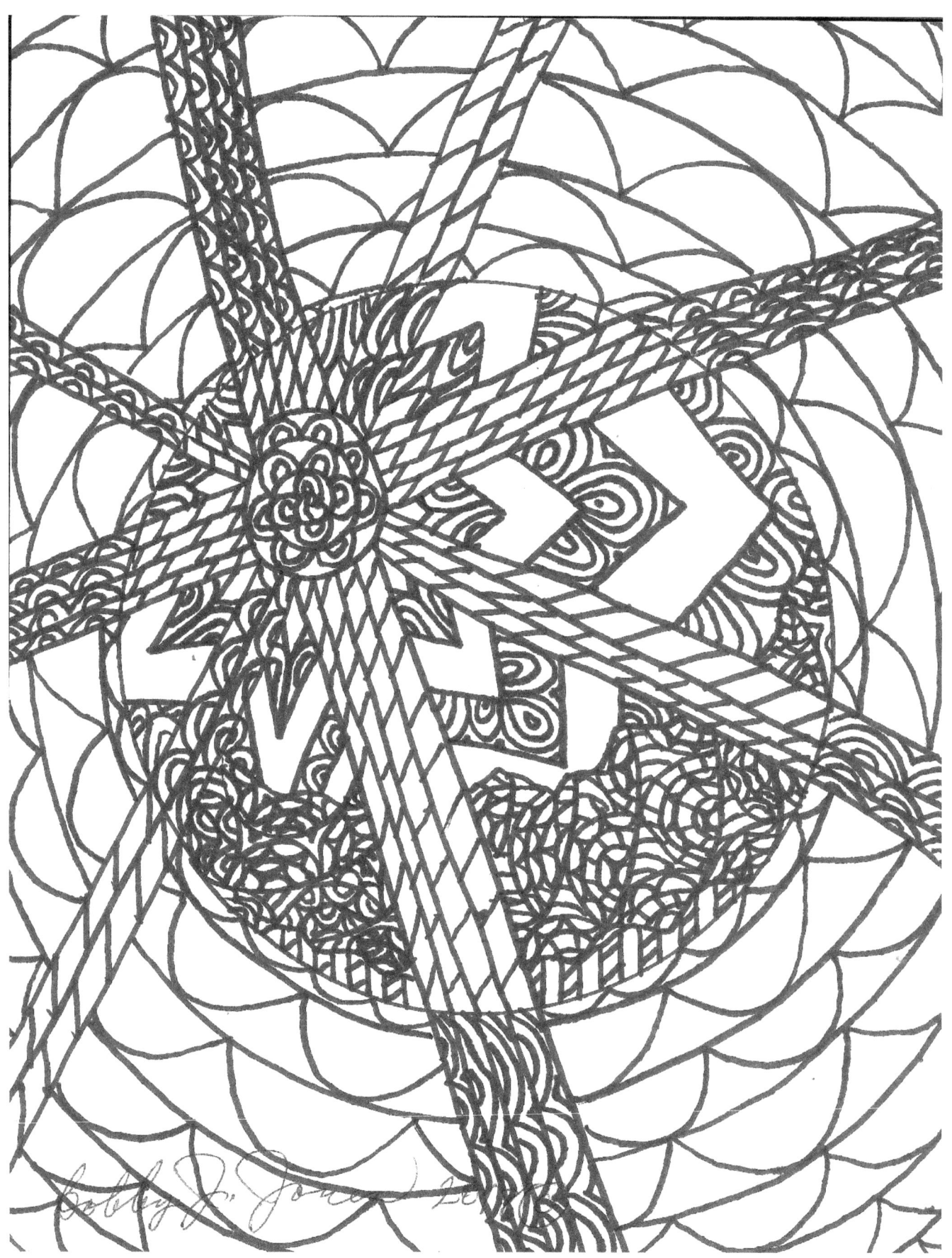

New Mexico Dreamscapes V

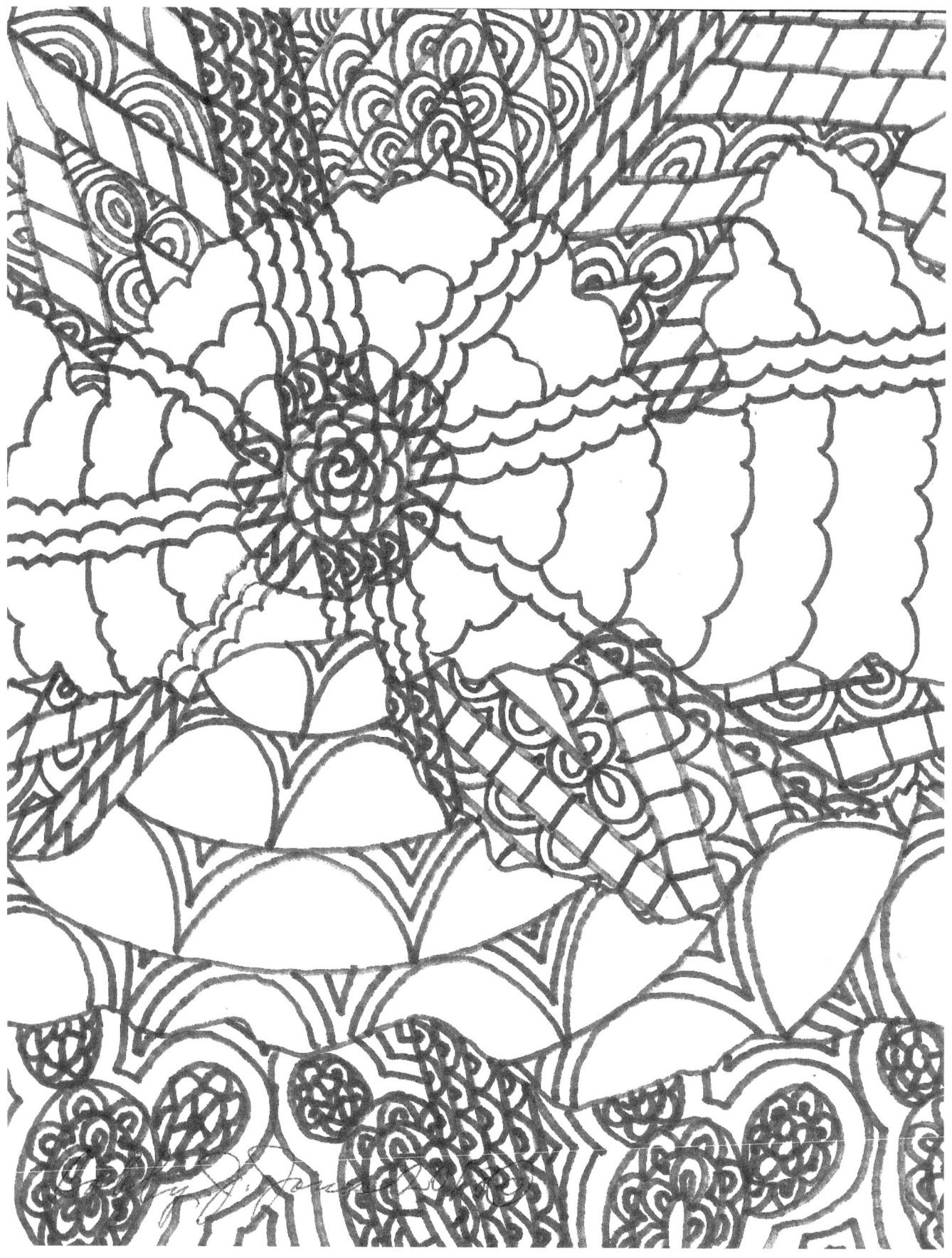

New Mexico Dreamscapes V

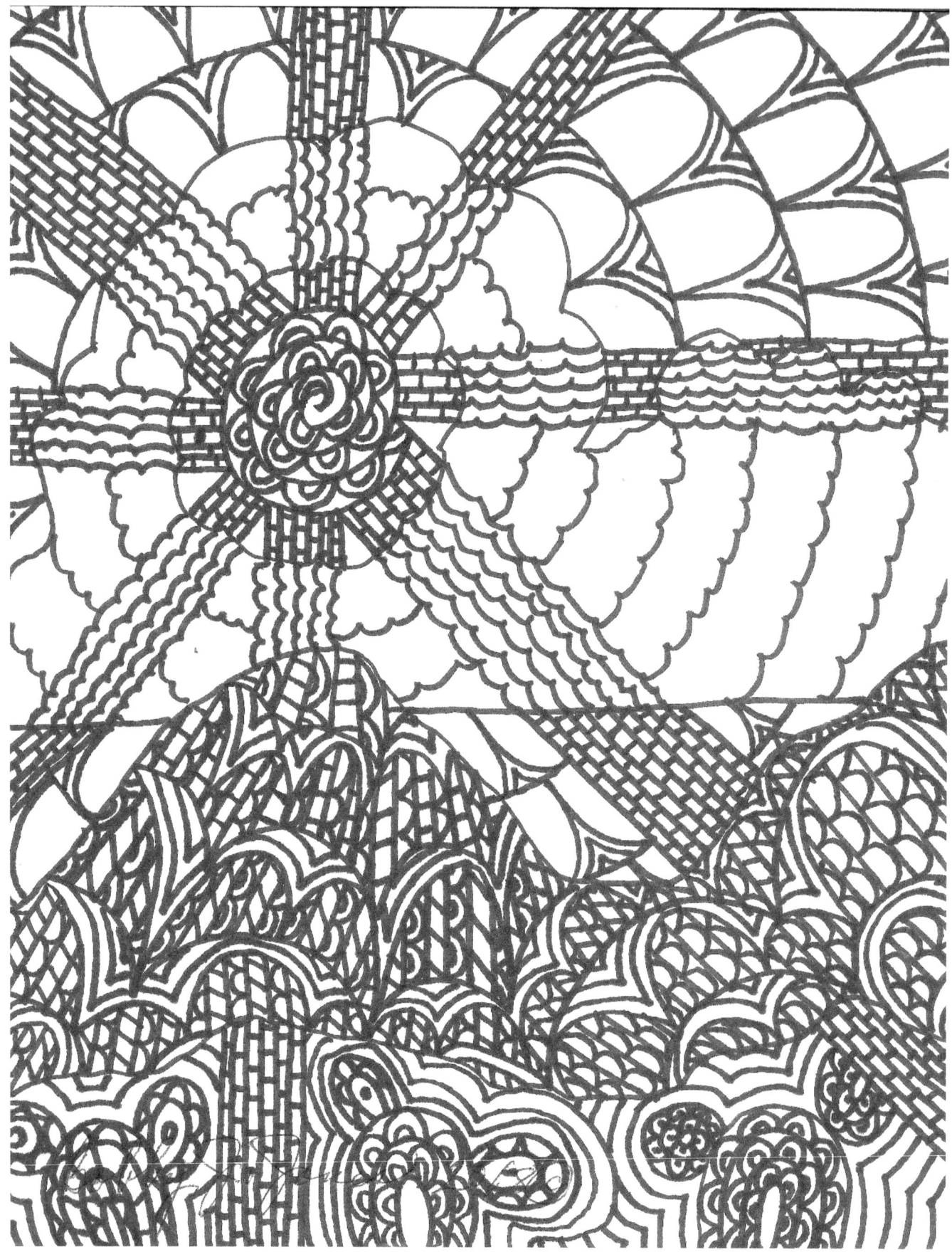

New Mexico Dreamscapes V

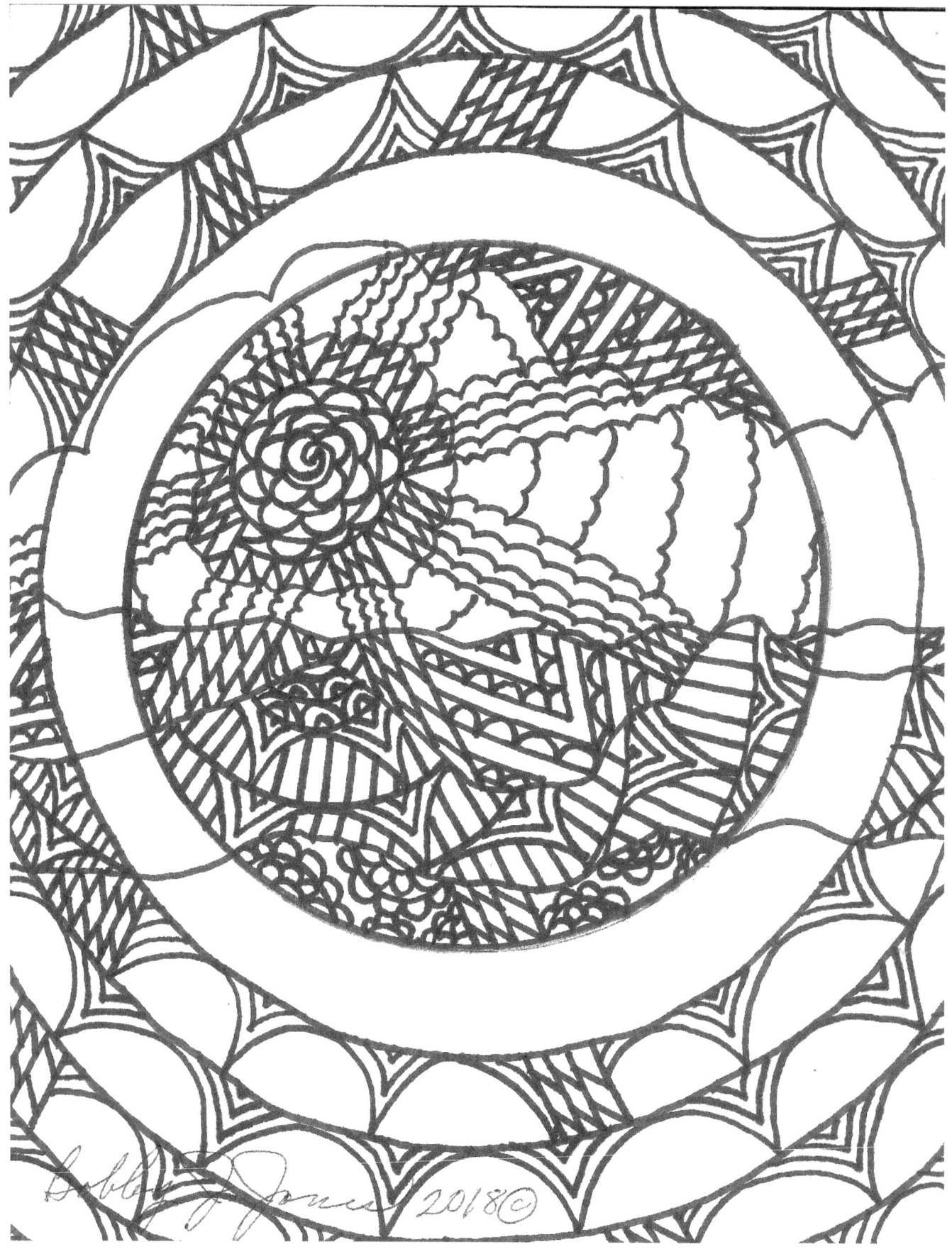

New Mexico Dreamscapes V

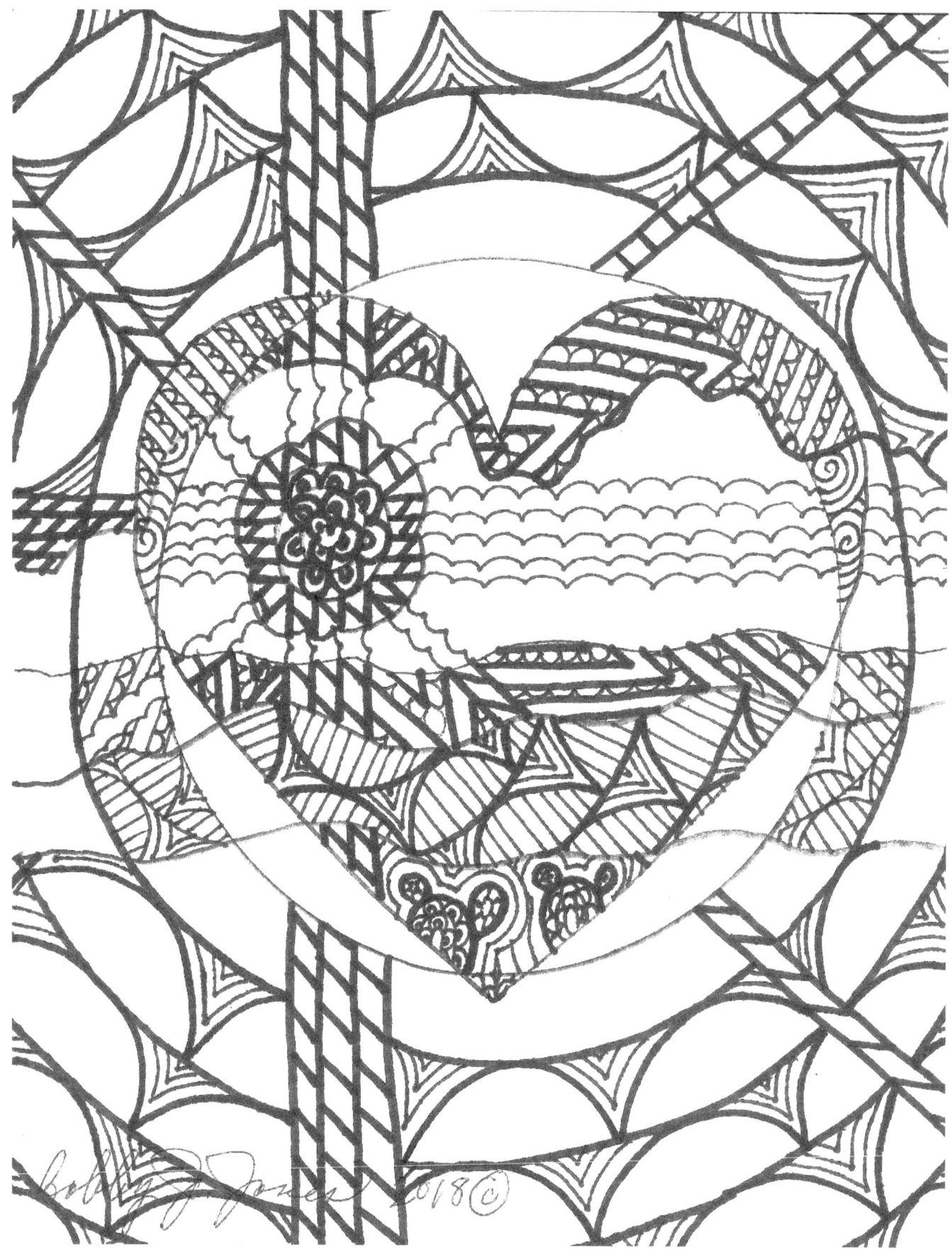

New Mexico Dreamscapes V

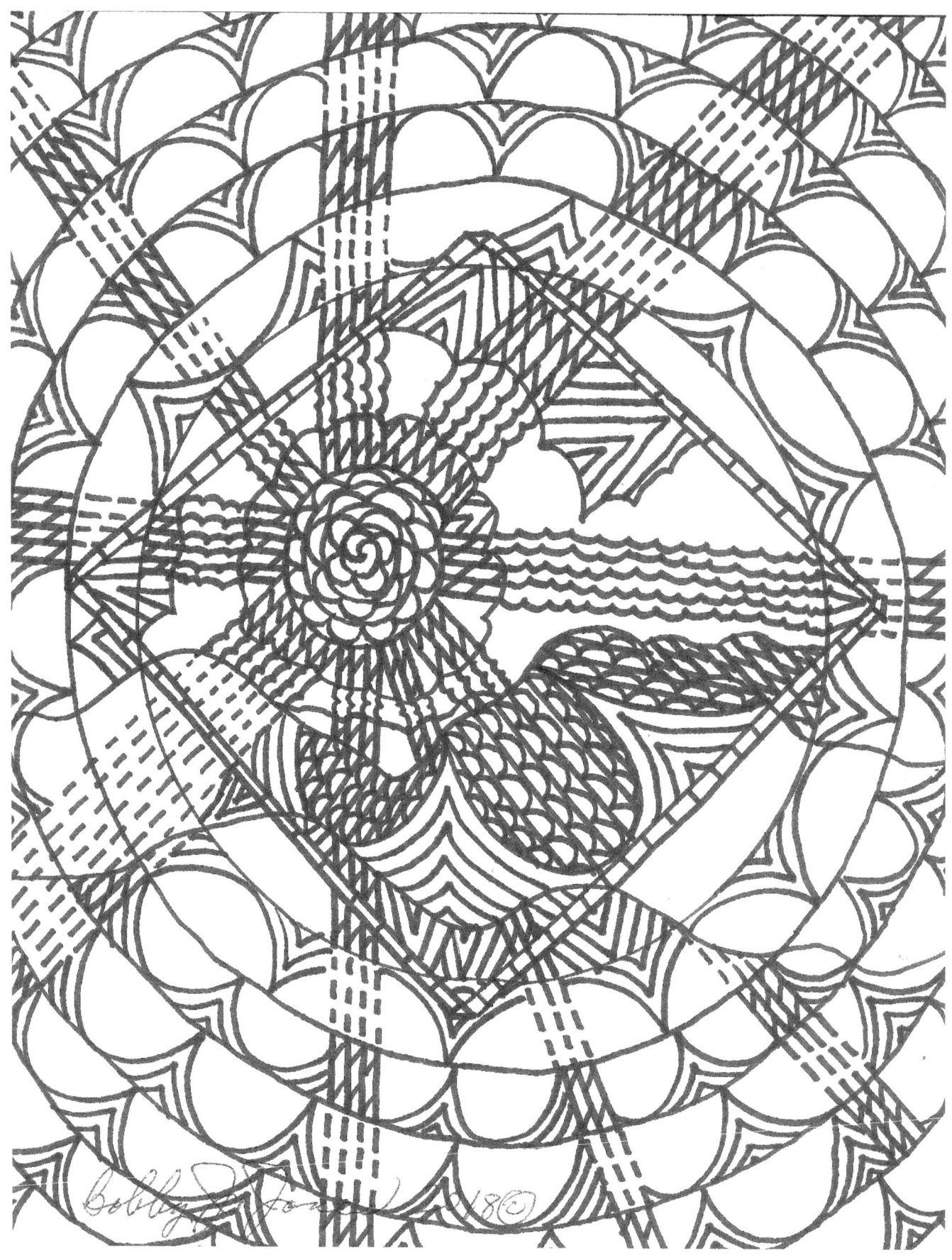

New Mexico Dreamscapes V

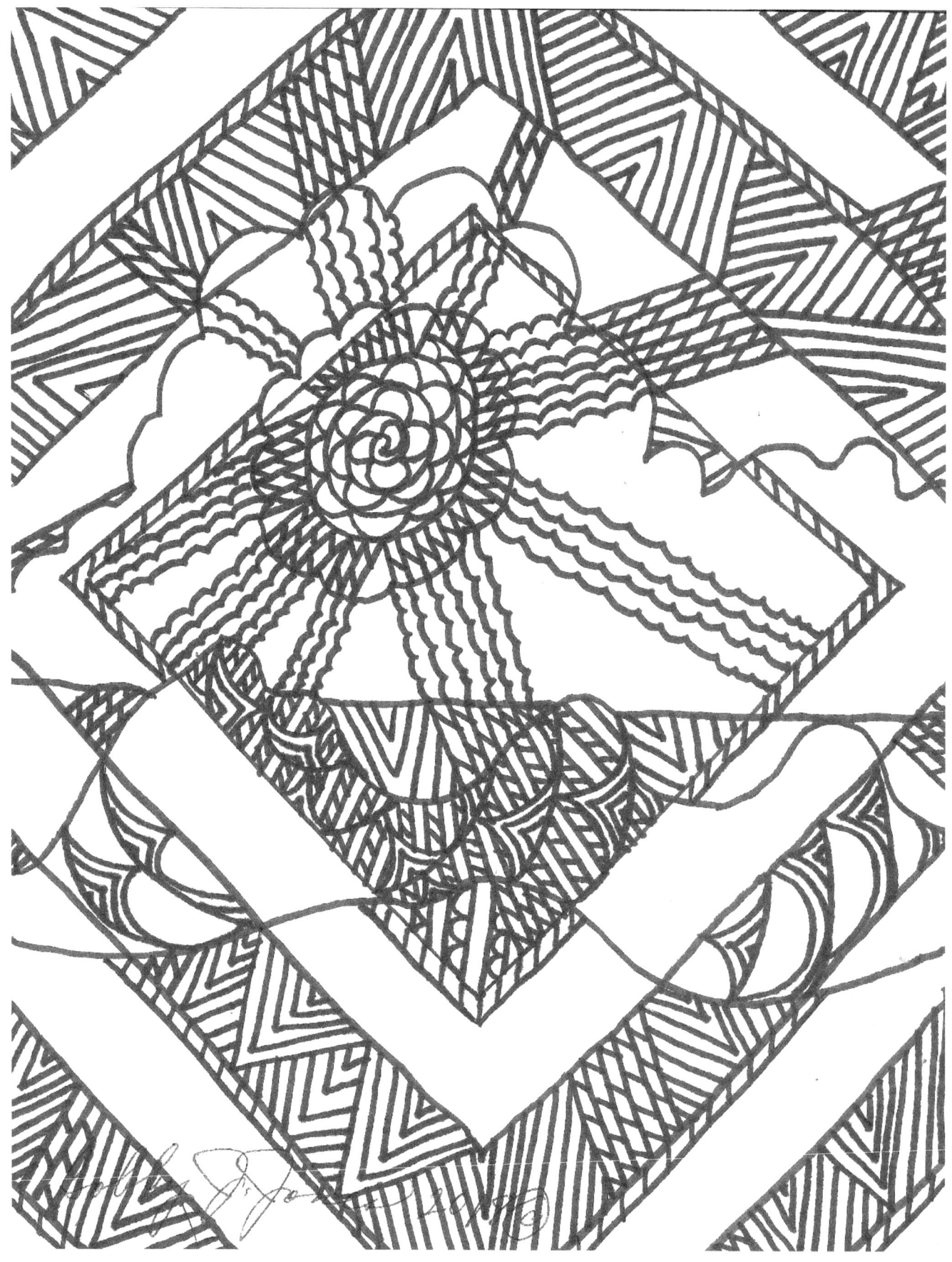

New Mexico Dreamscapes V

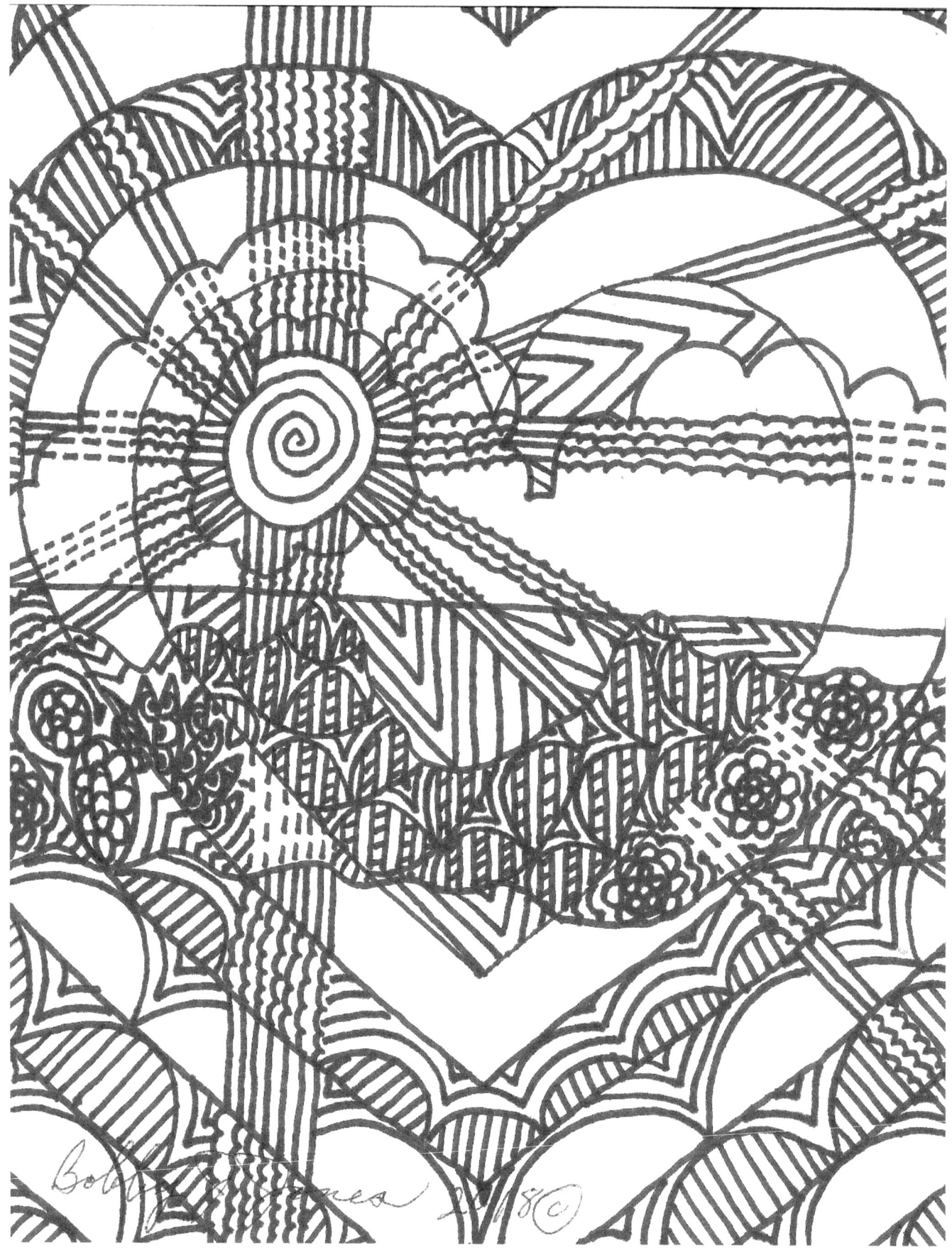

New Mexico Dreamscapes V

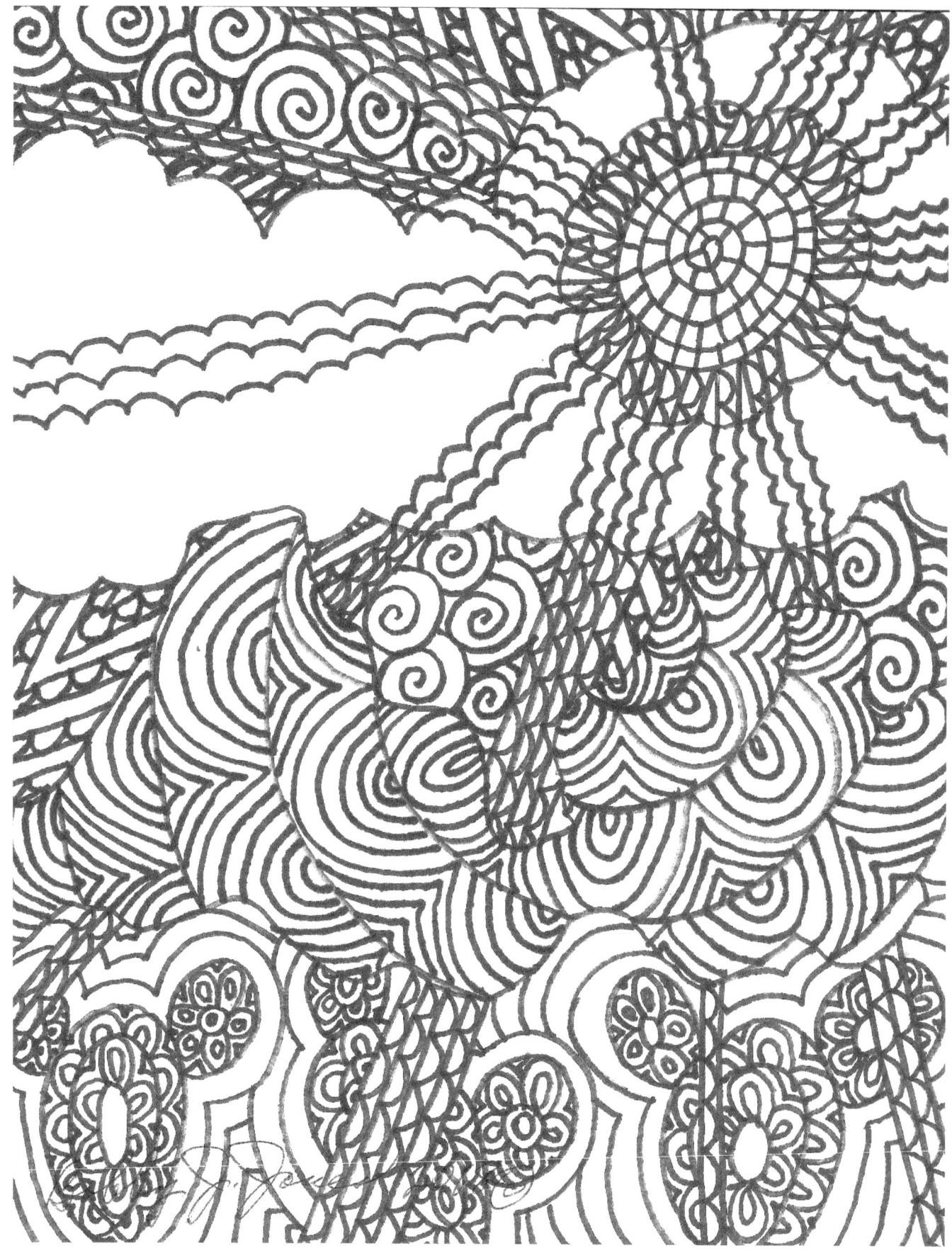

New Mexico Dreamscapes V

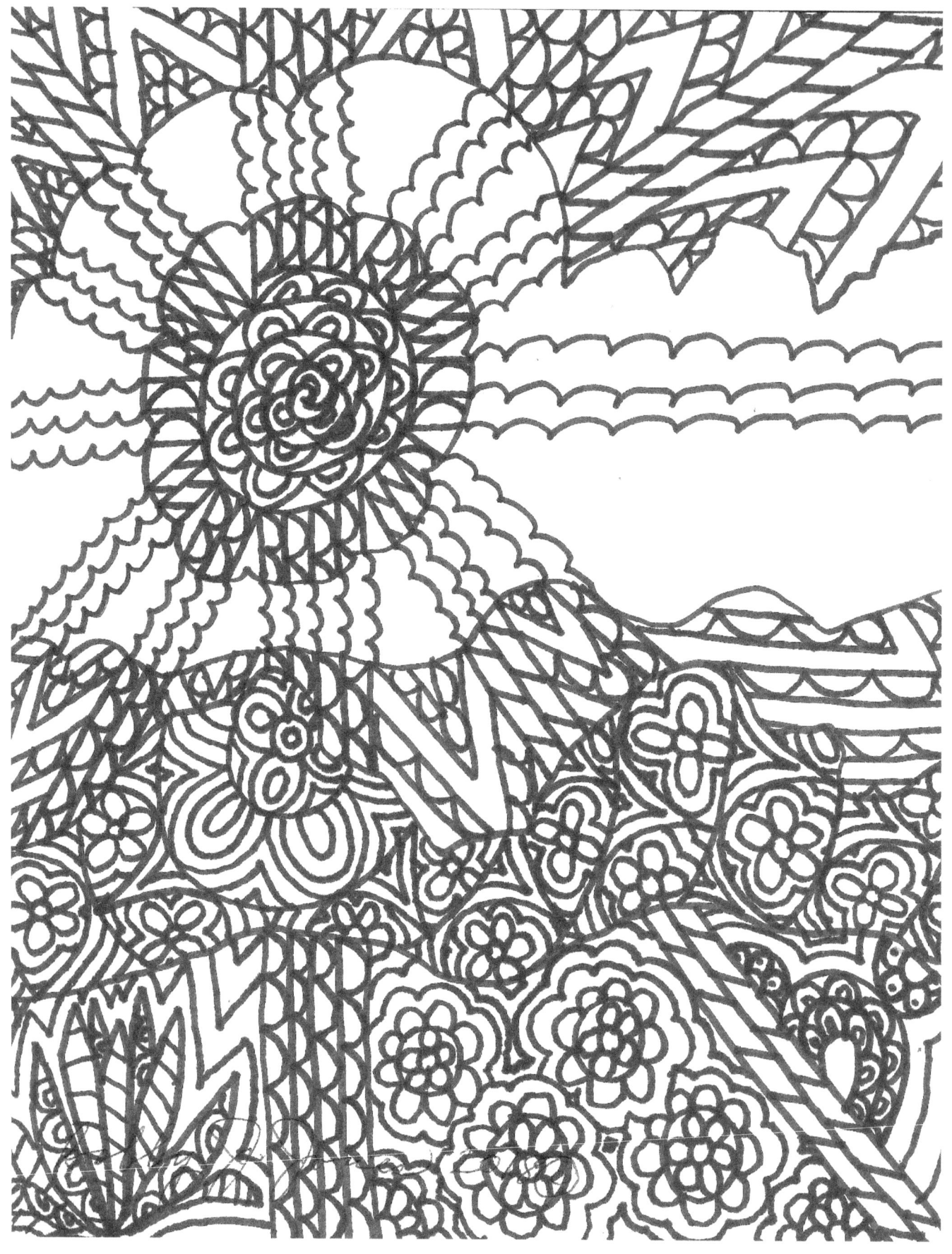

New Mexico Dreamscapes V

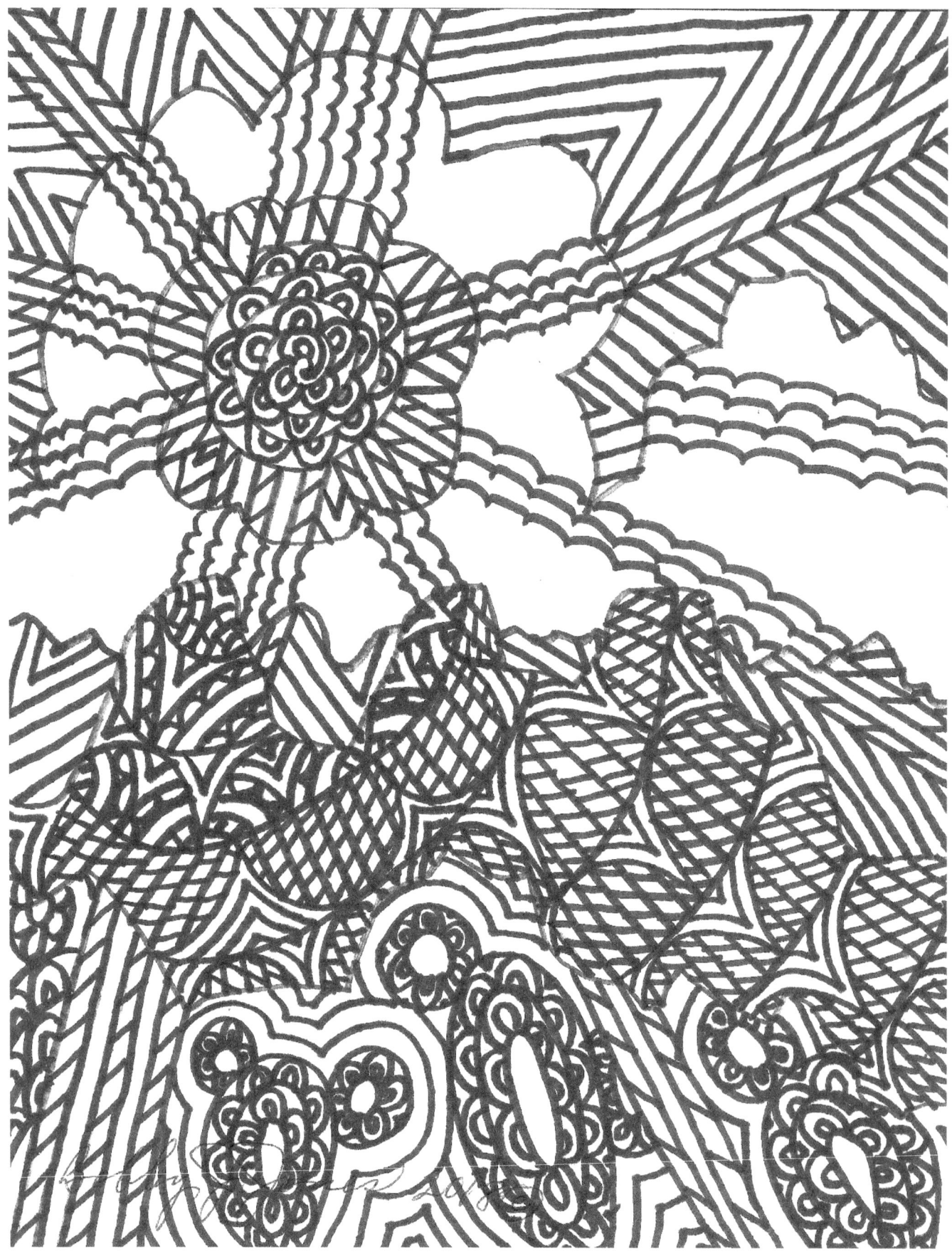

New Mexico Dreamscapes V

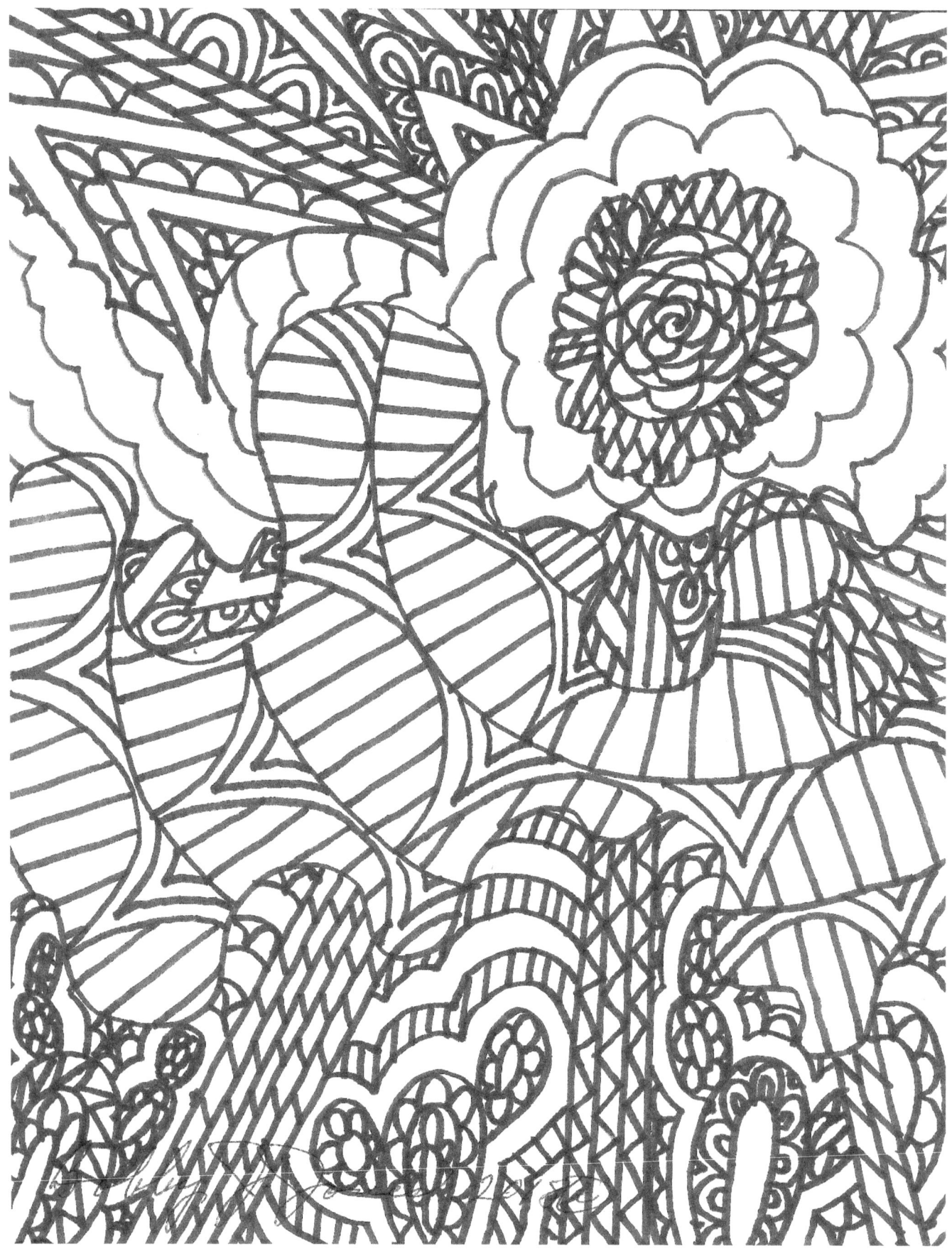

New Mexico Dreamscapes V

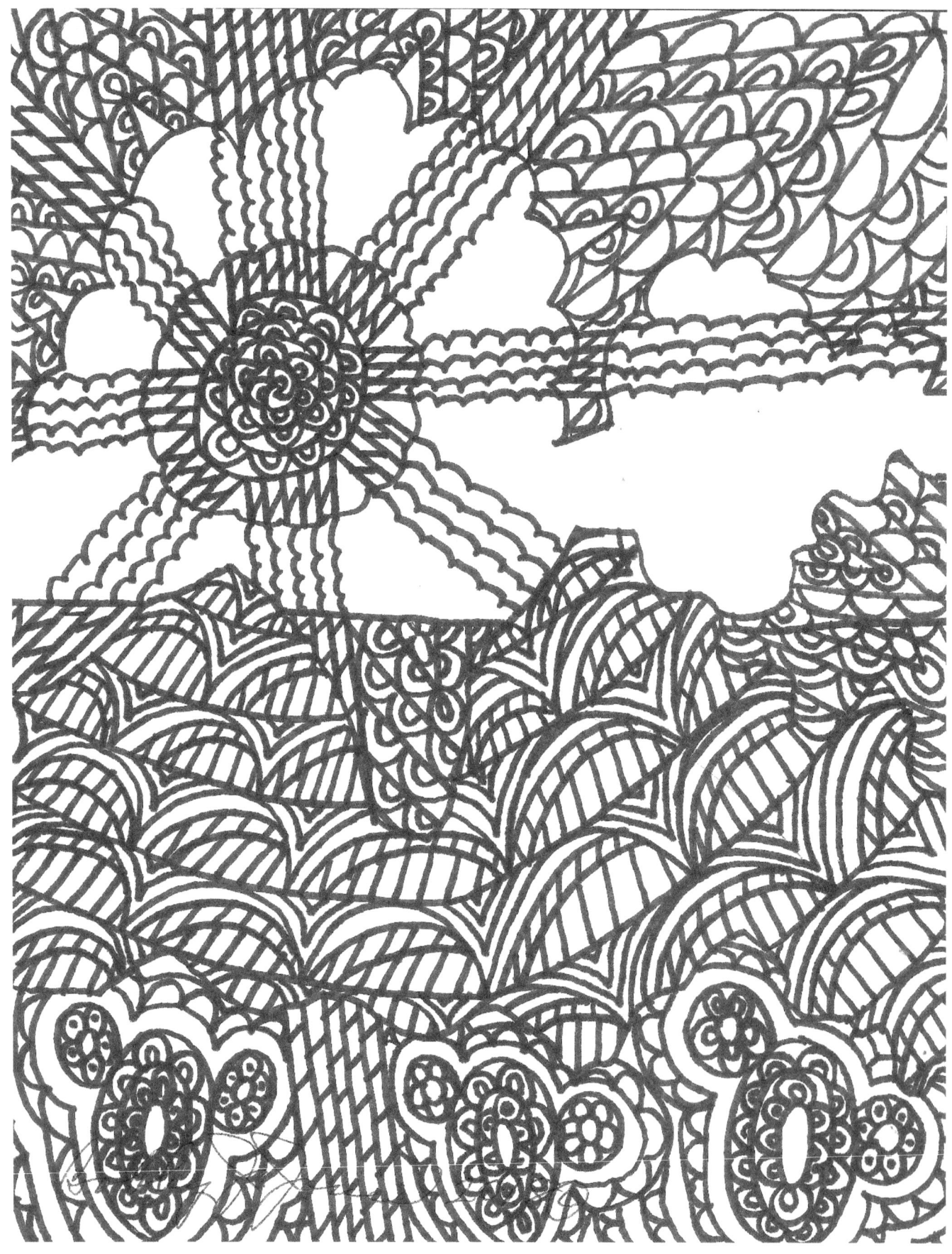

New Mexico Dreamscapes V

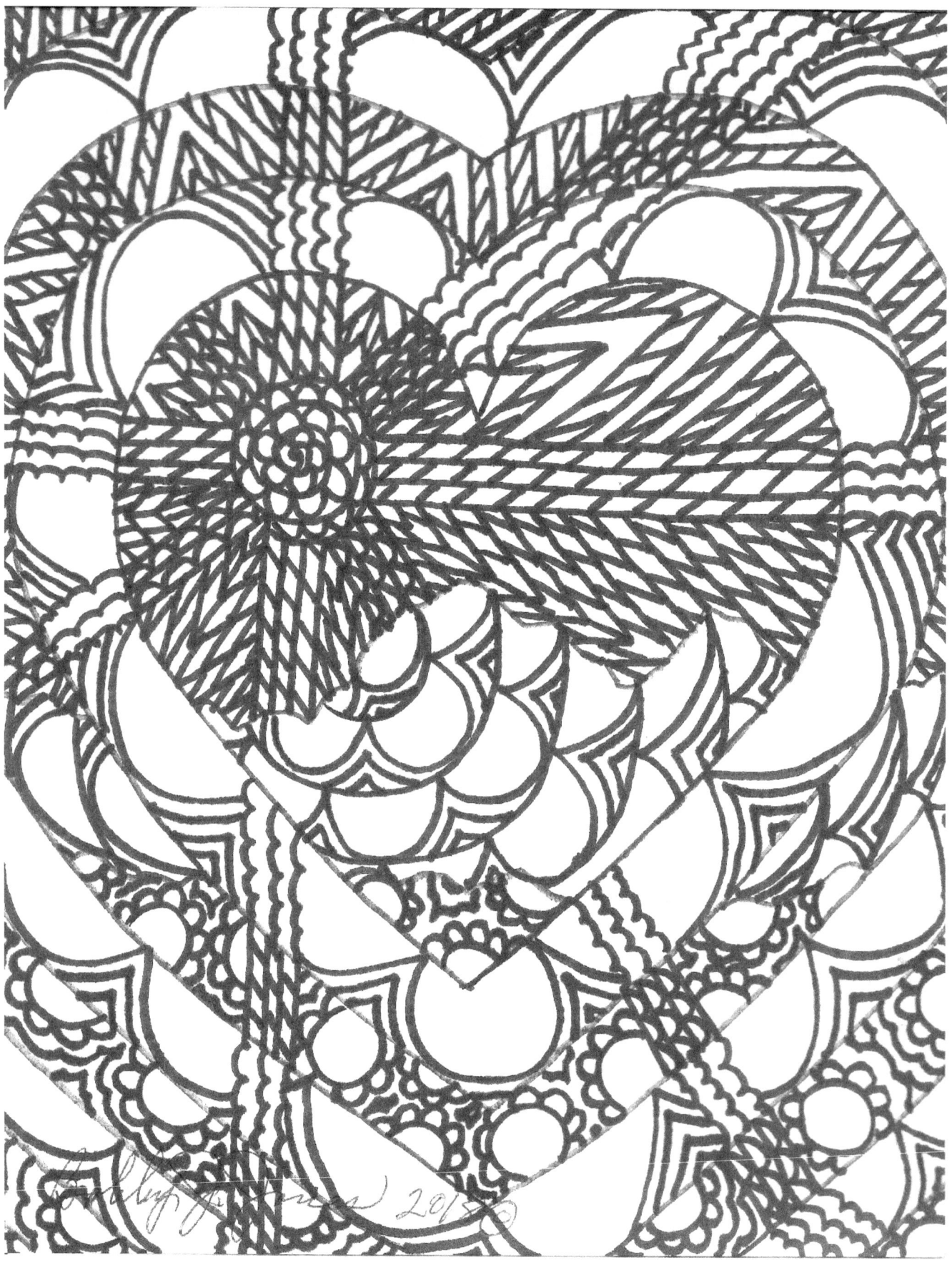

New Mexico Dreamscapes V

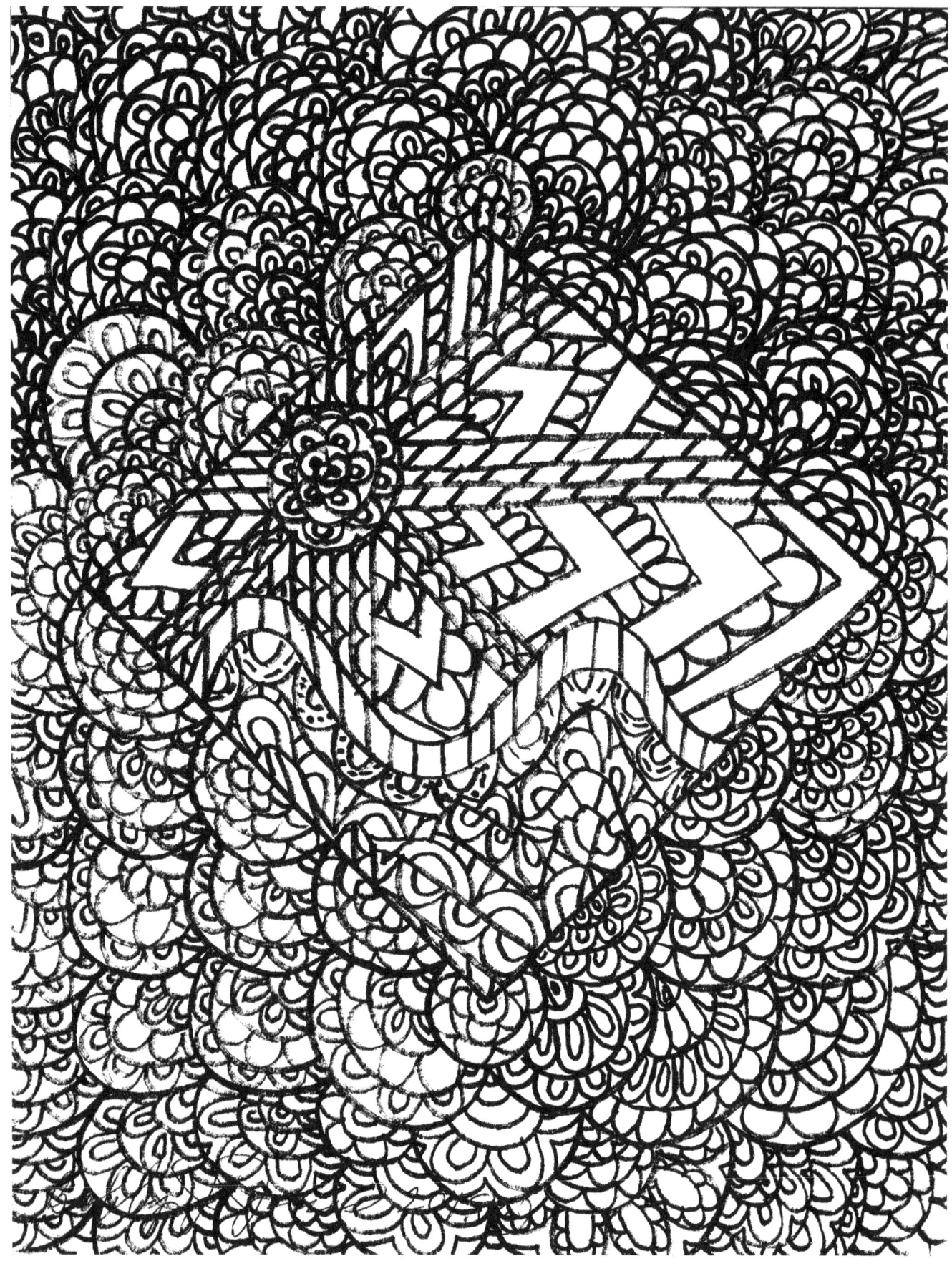

New Mexico Dreamscapes V

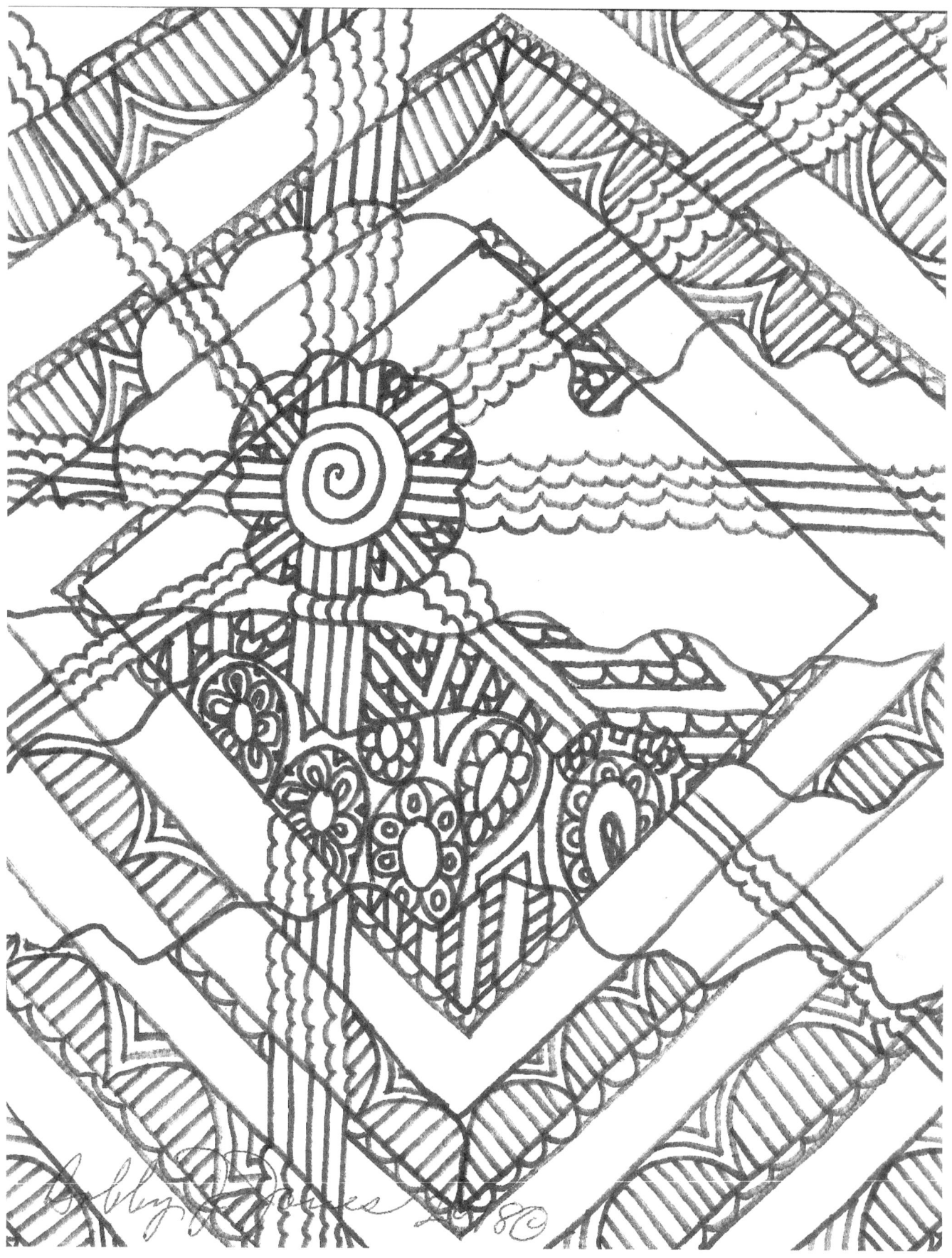

New Mexico Dreamscapes V

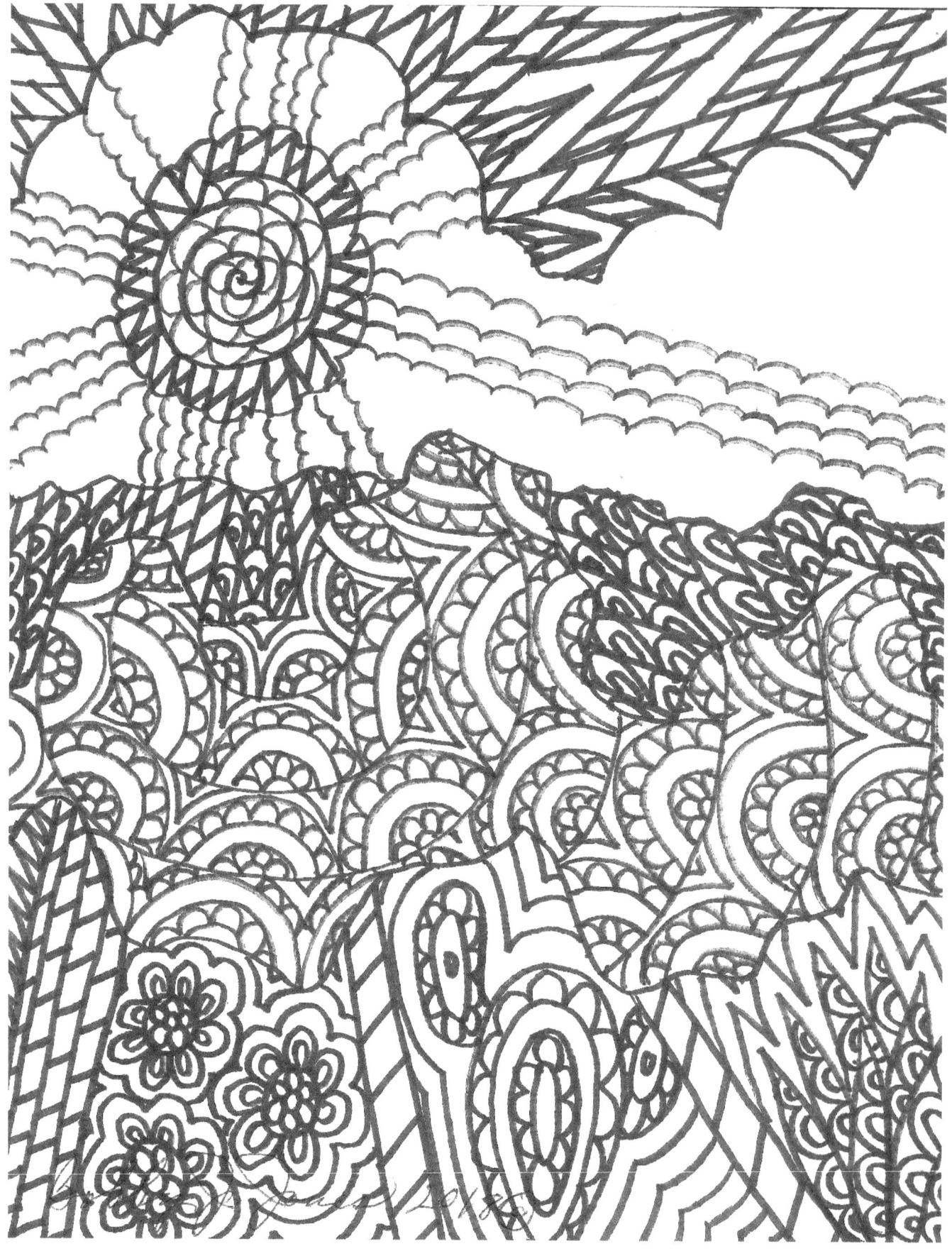

New Mexico Dreamscapes V

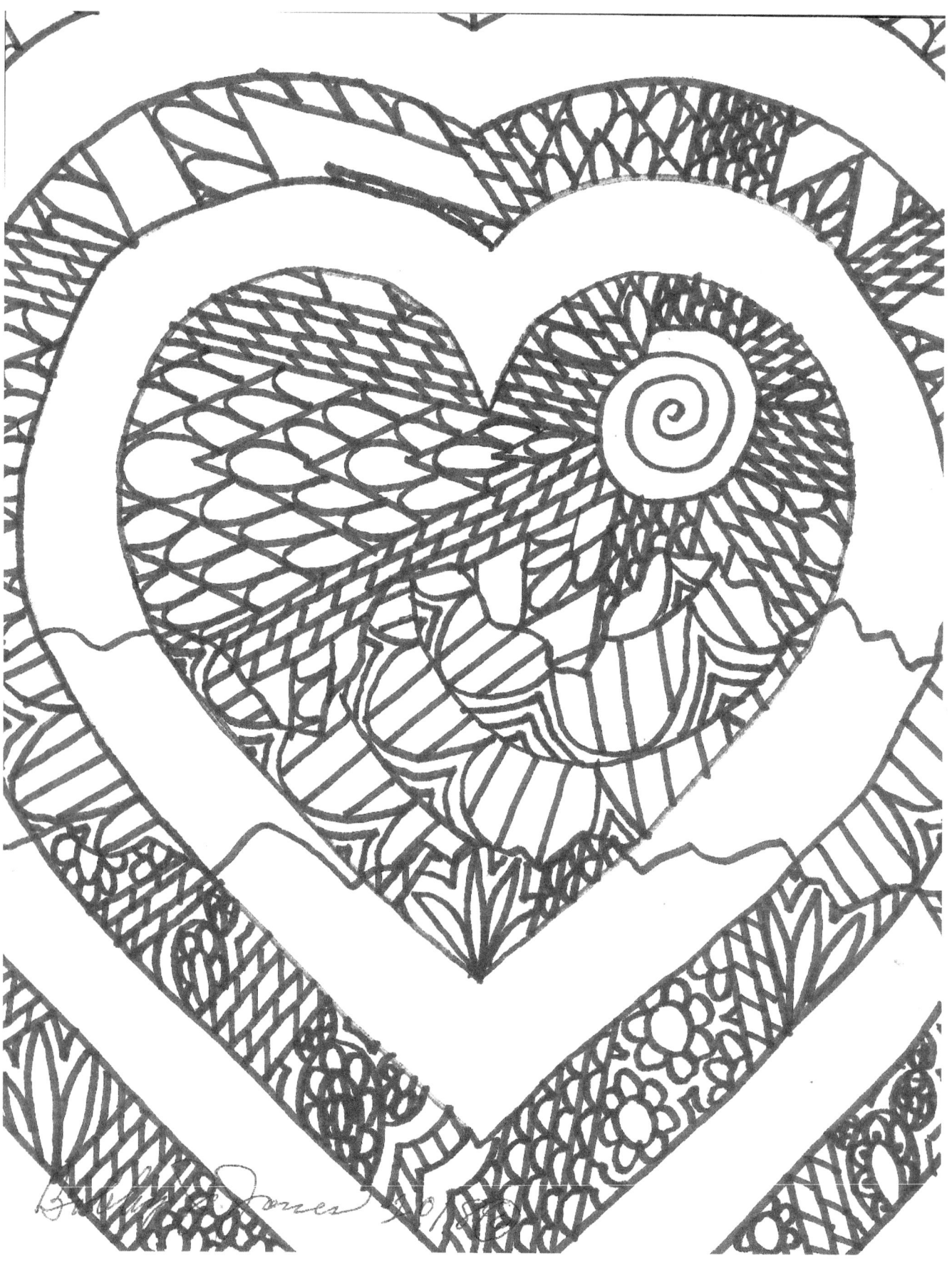

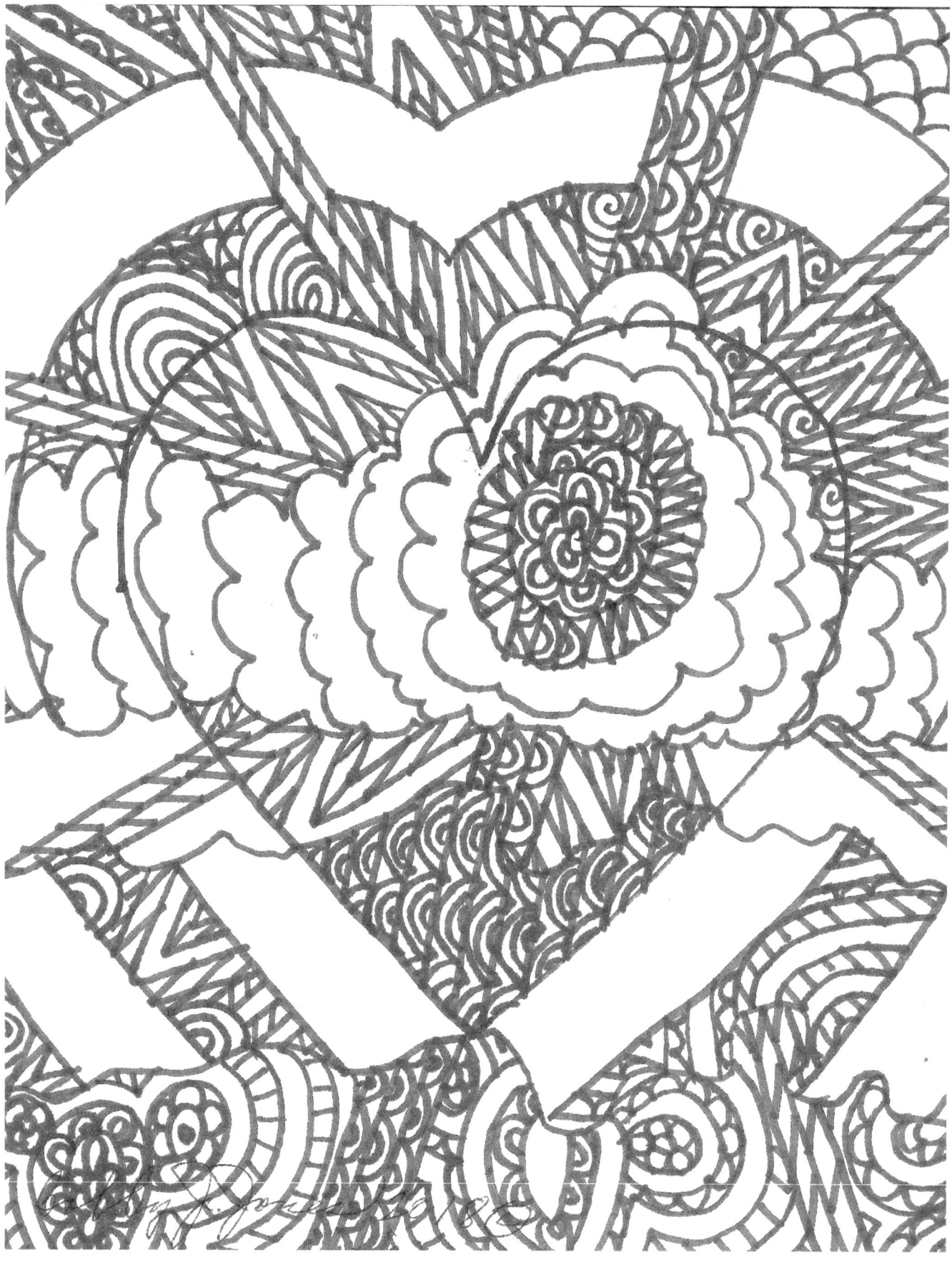

New Mexico Dreamscapes V

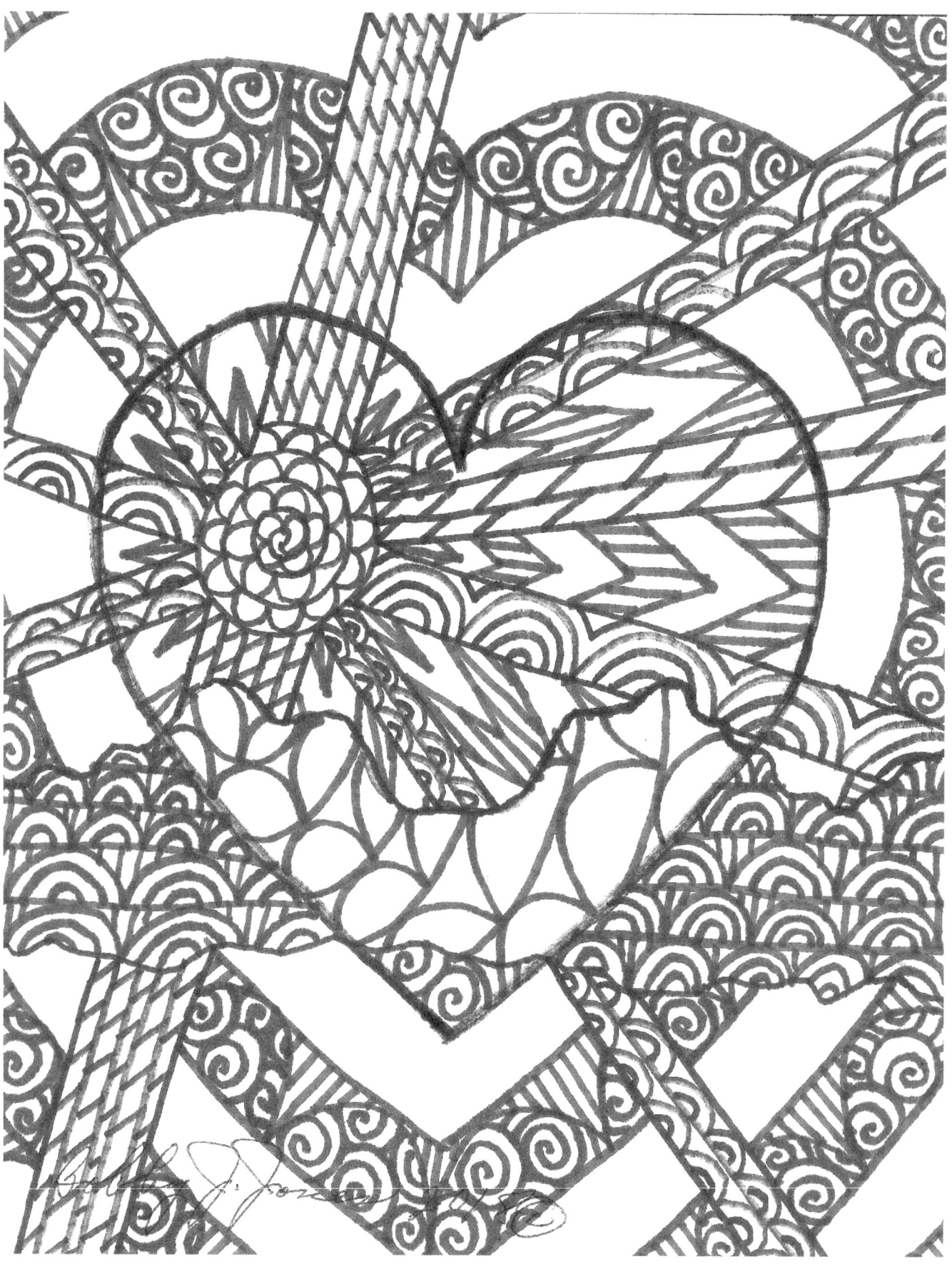

New Mexico Dreamscapes V

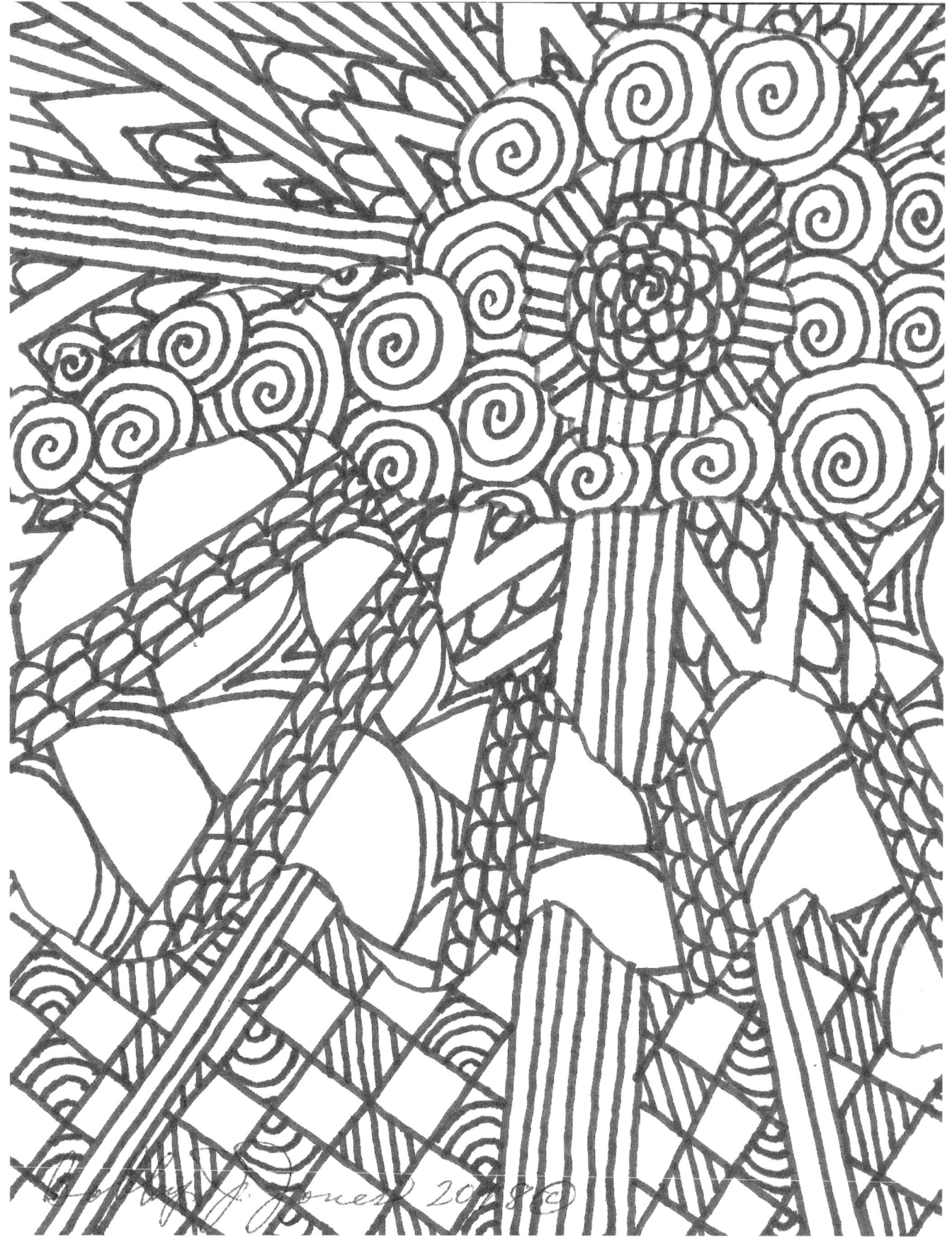

New Mexico Dreamscapes V

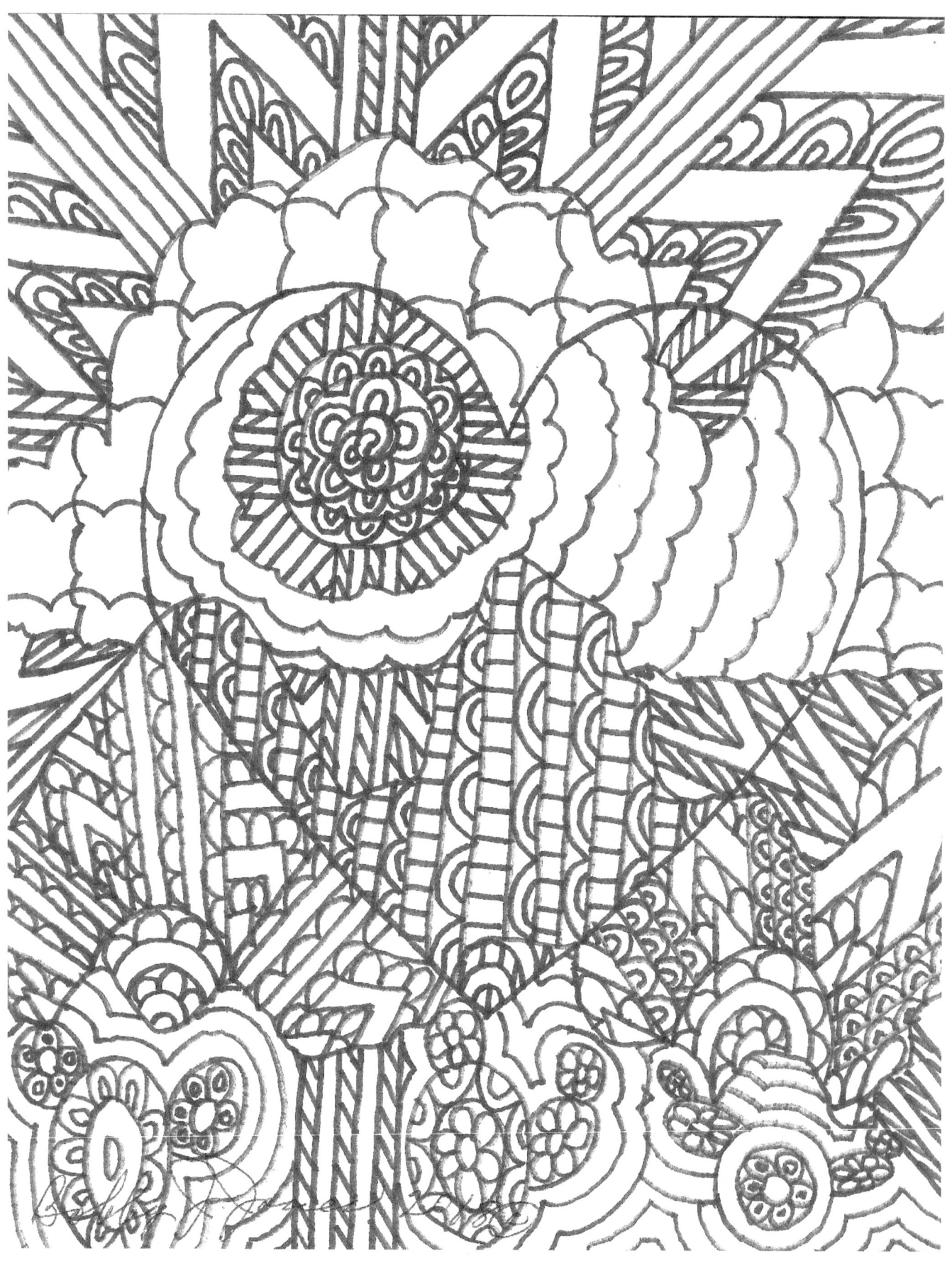

New Mexico Dreamscapes V

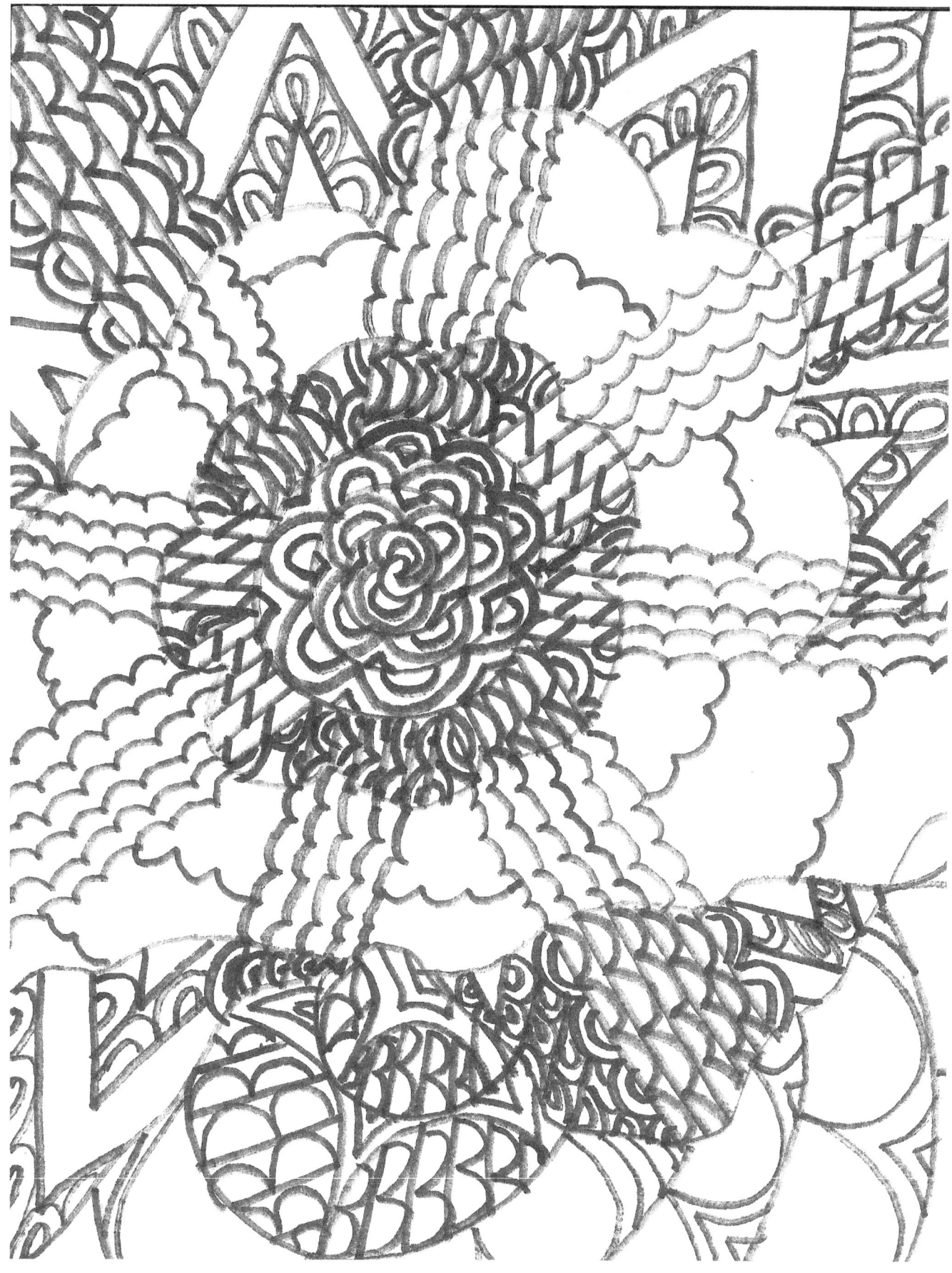

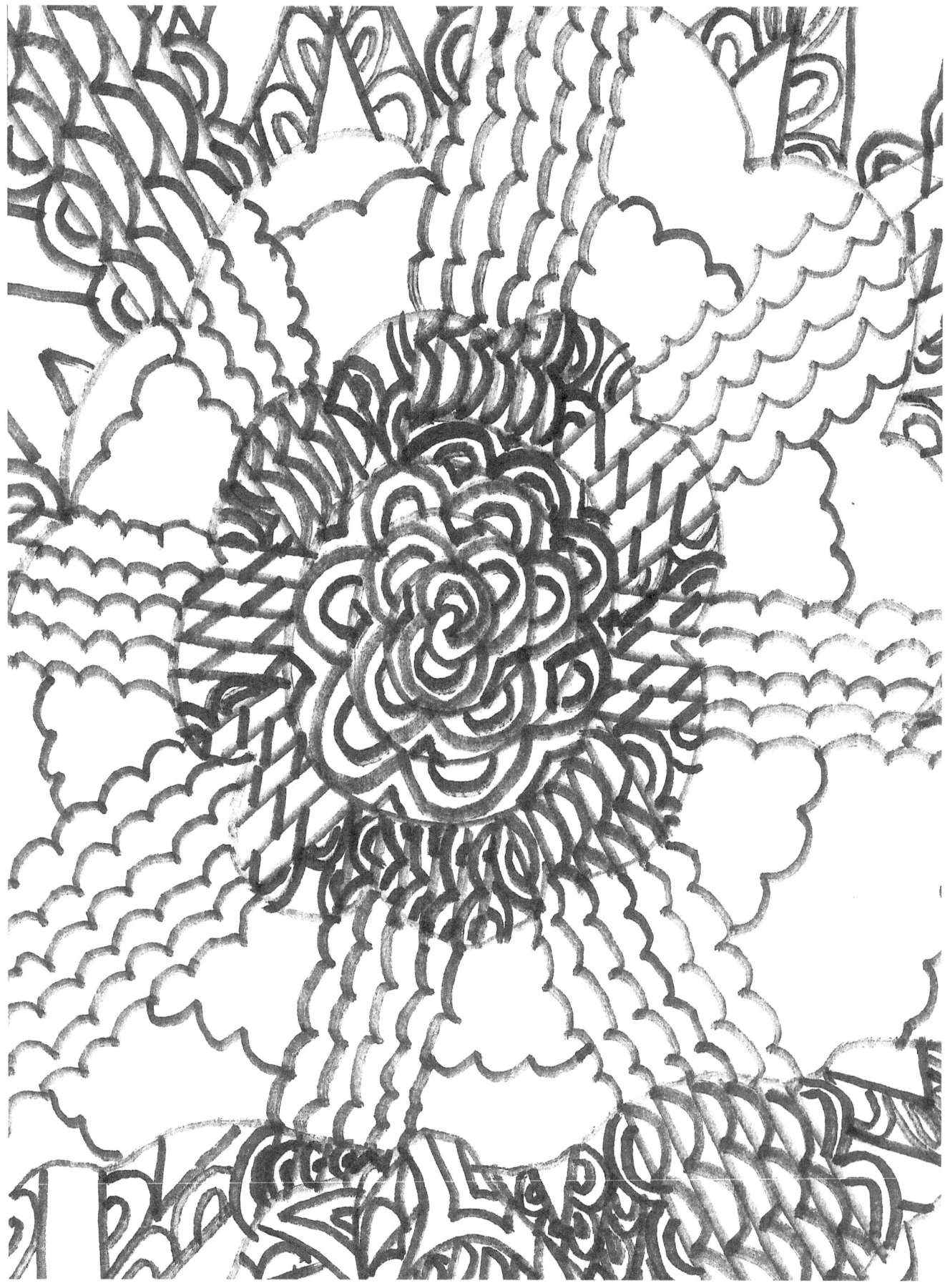

New Mexico Dreamscapes V

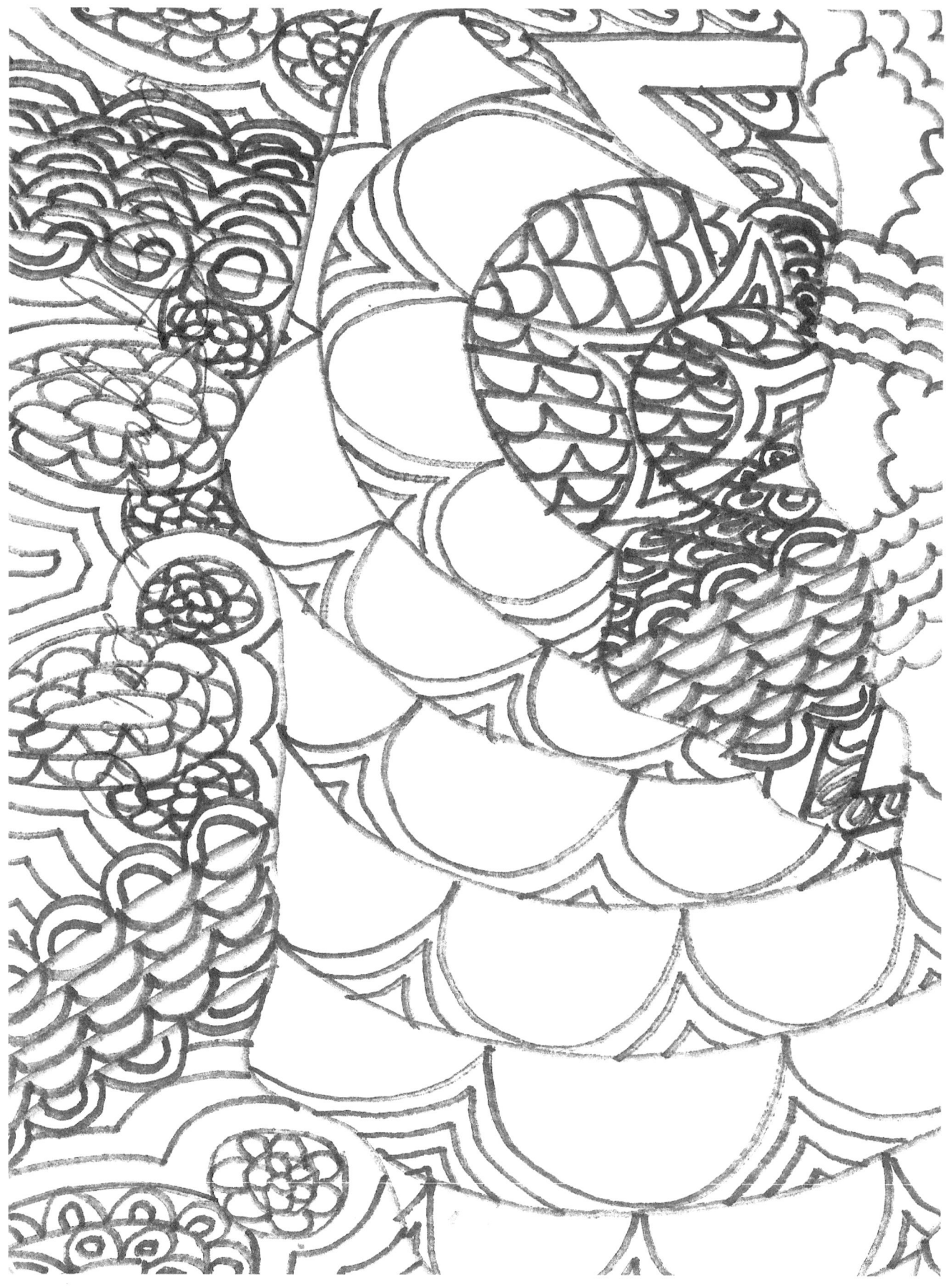

New Mexico Dreamscapes V

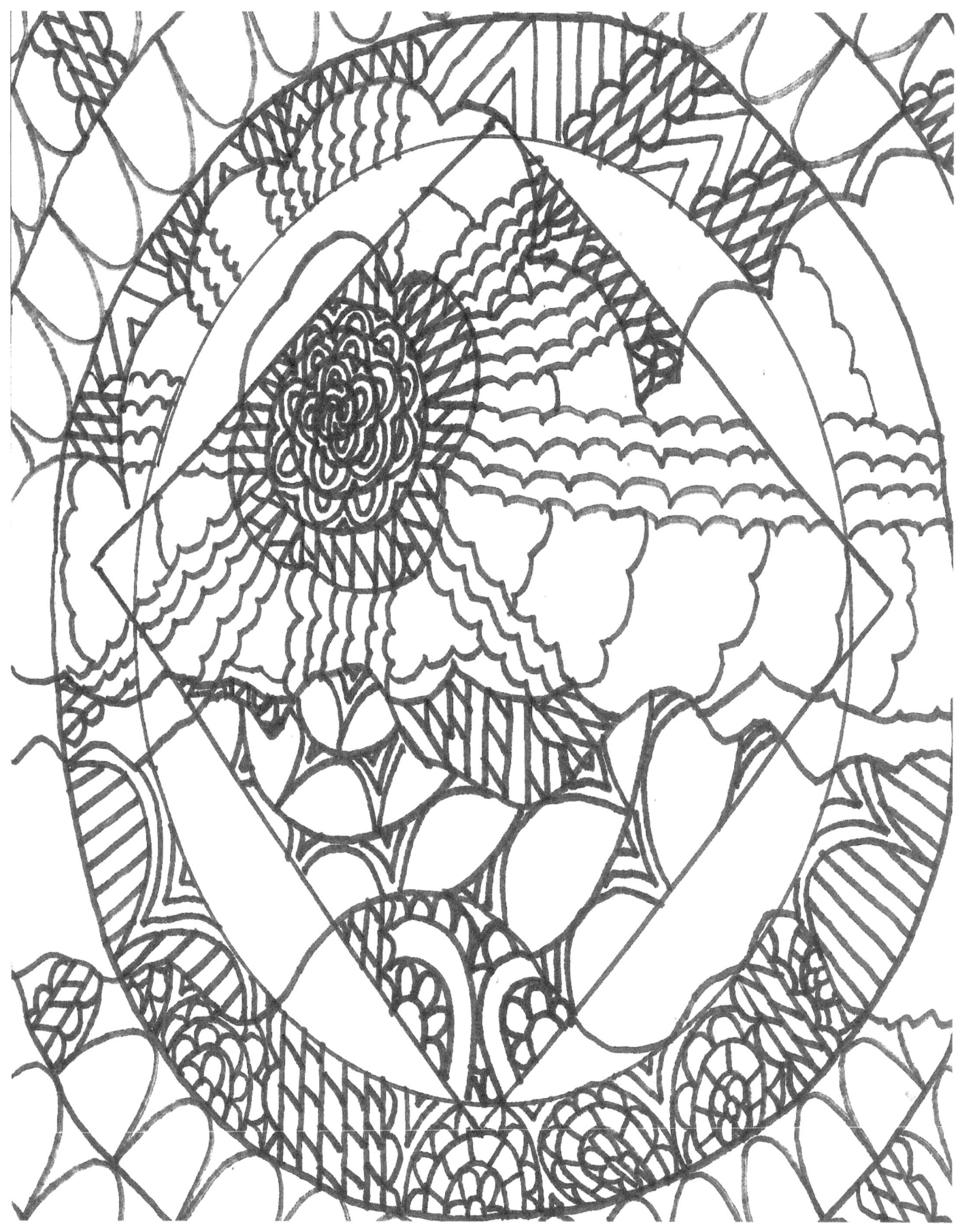

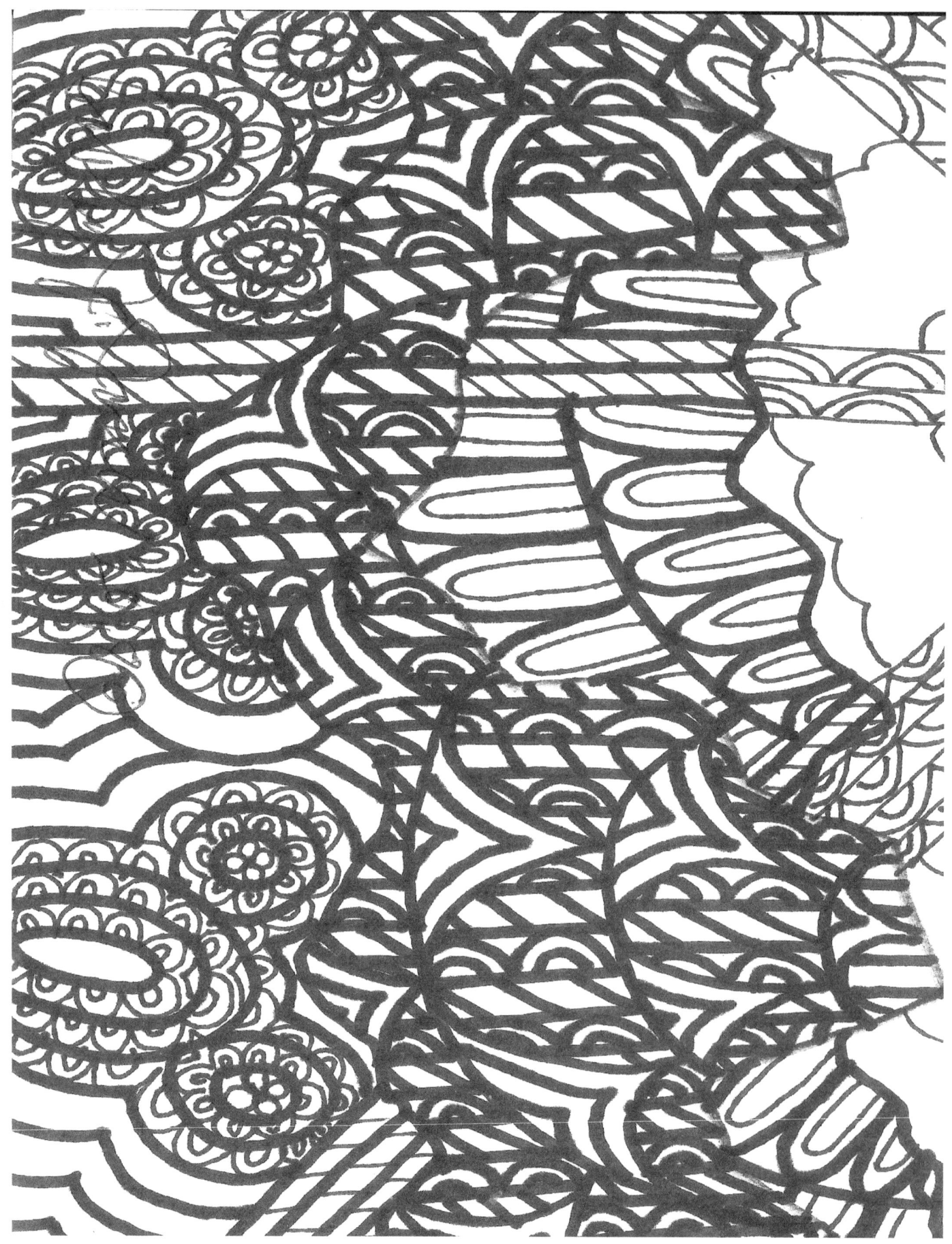

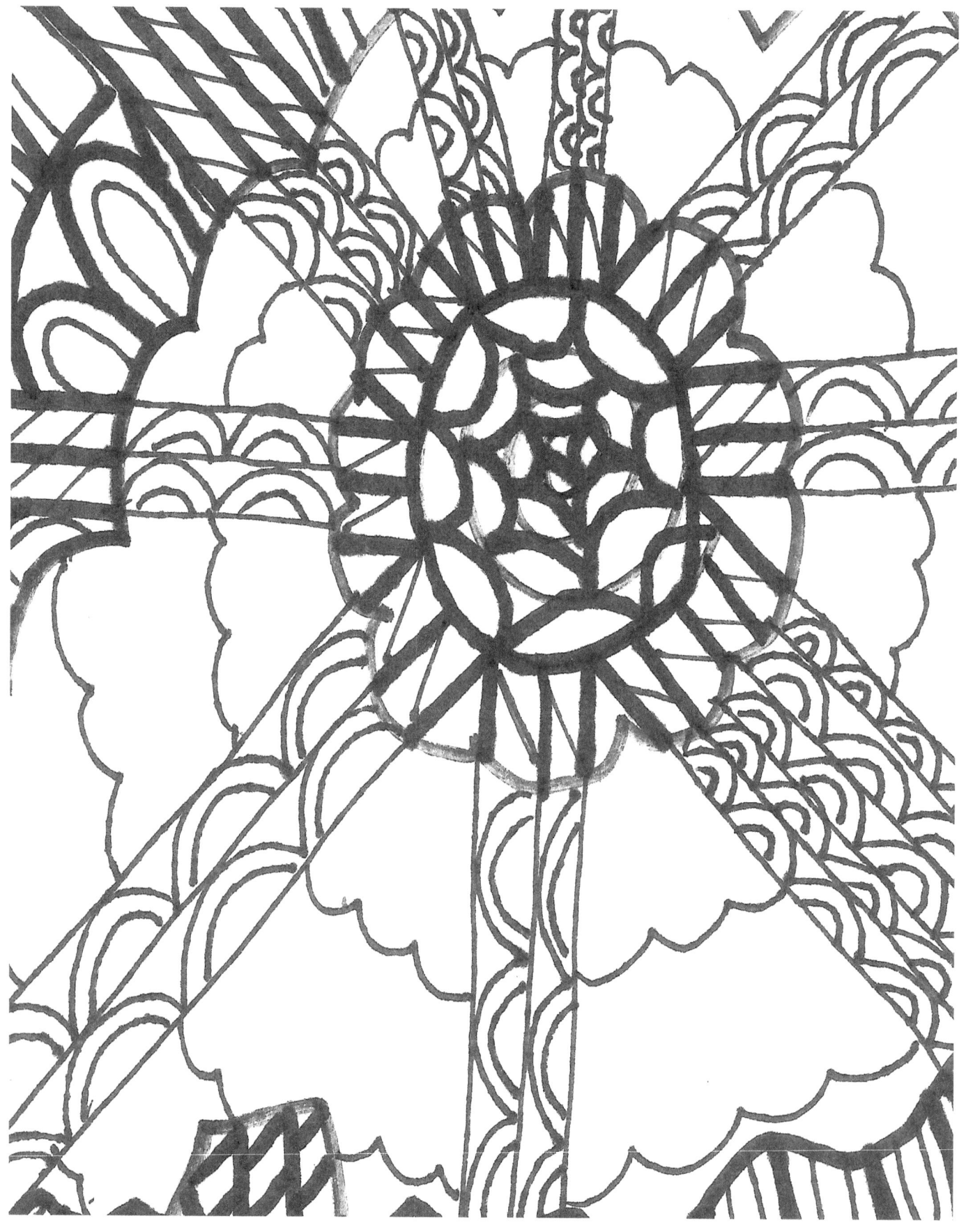

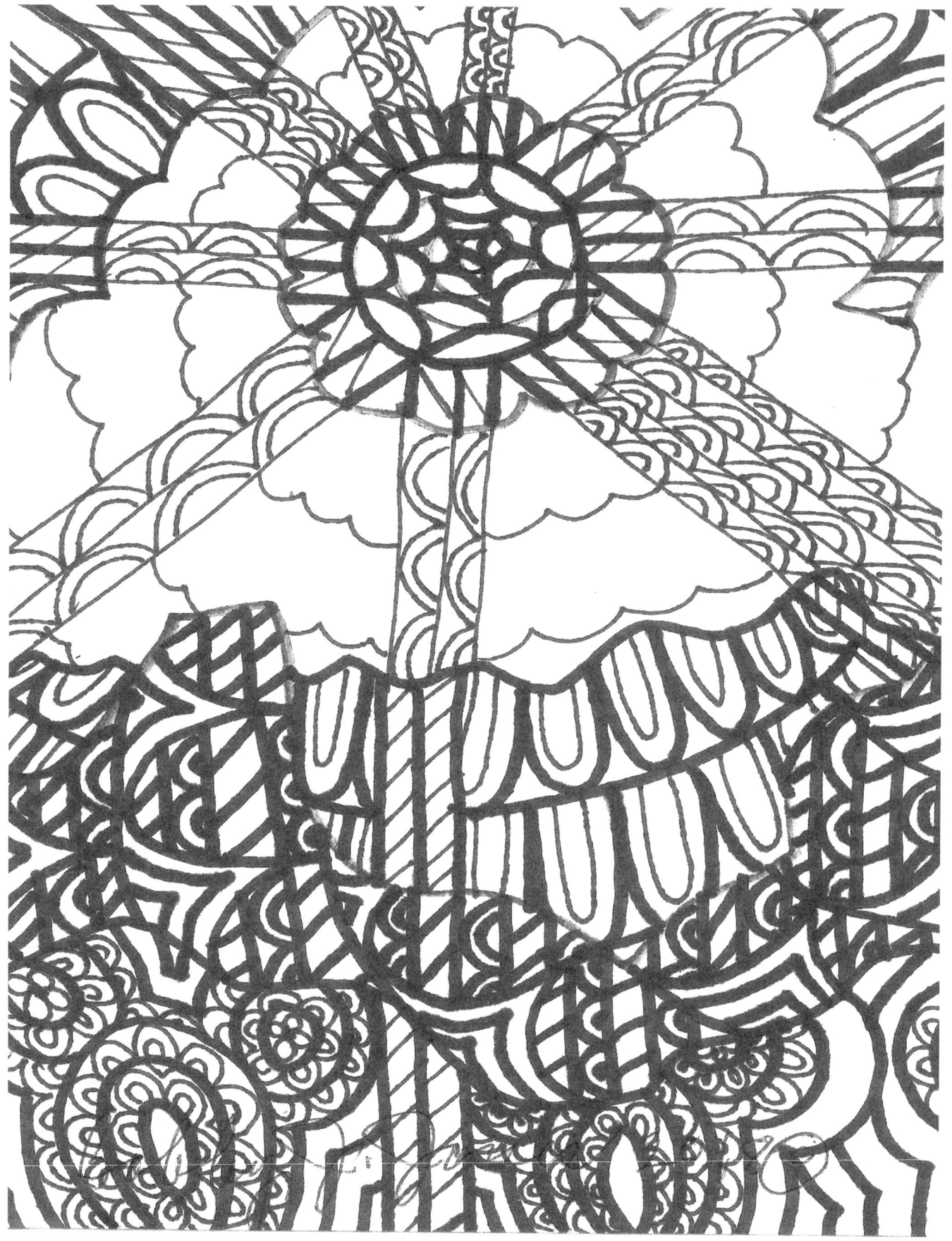

New Mexico Dreamscapes V

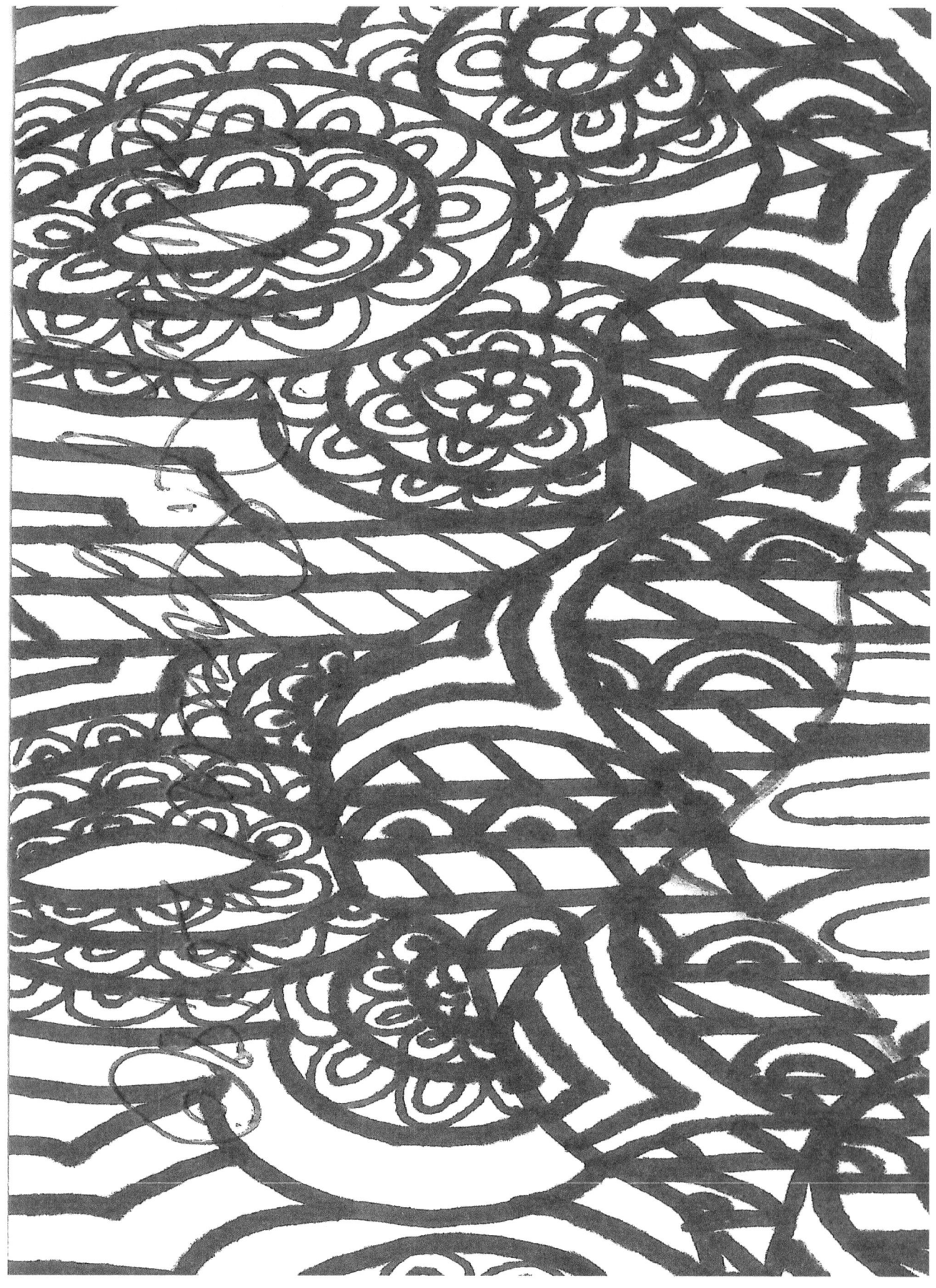

New Mexico Dreamscapes V

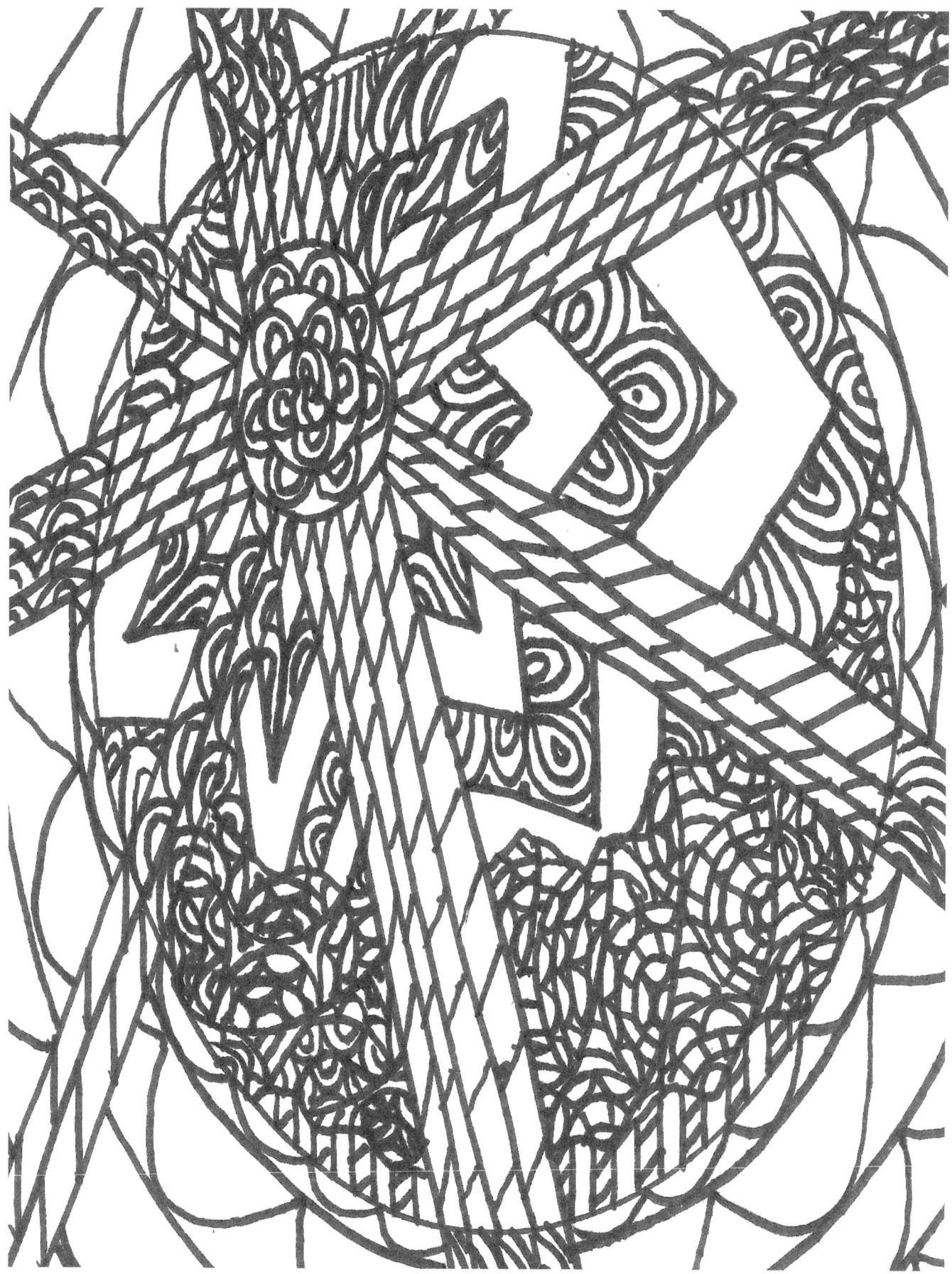

New Mexico Dreamscapes V

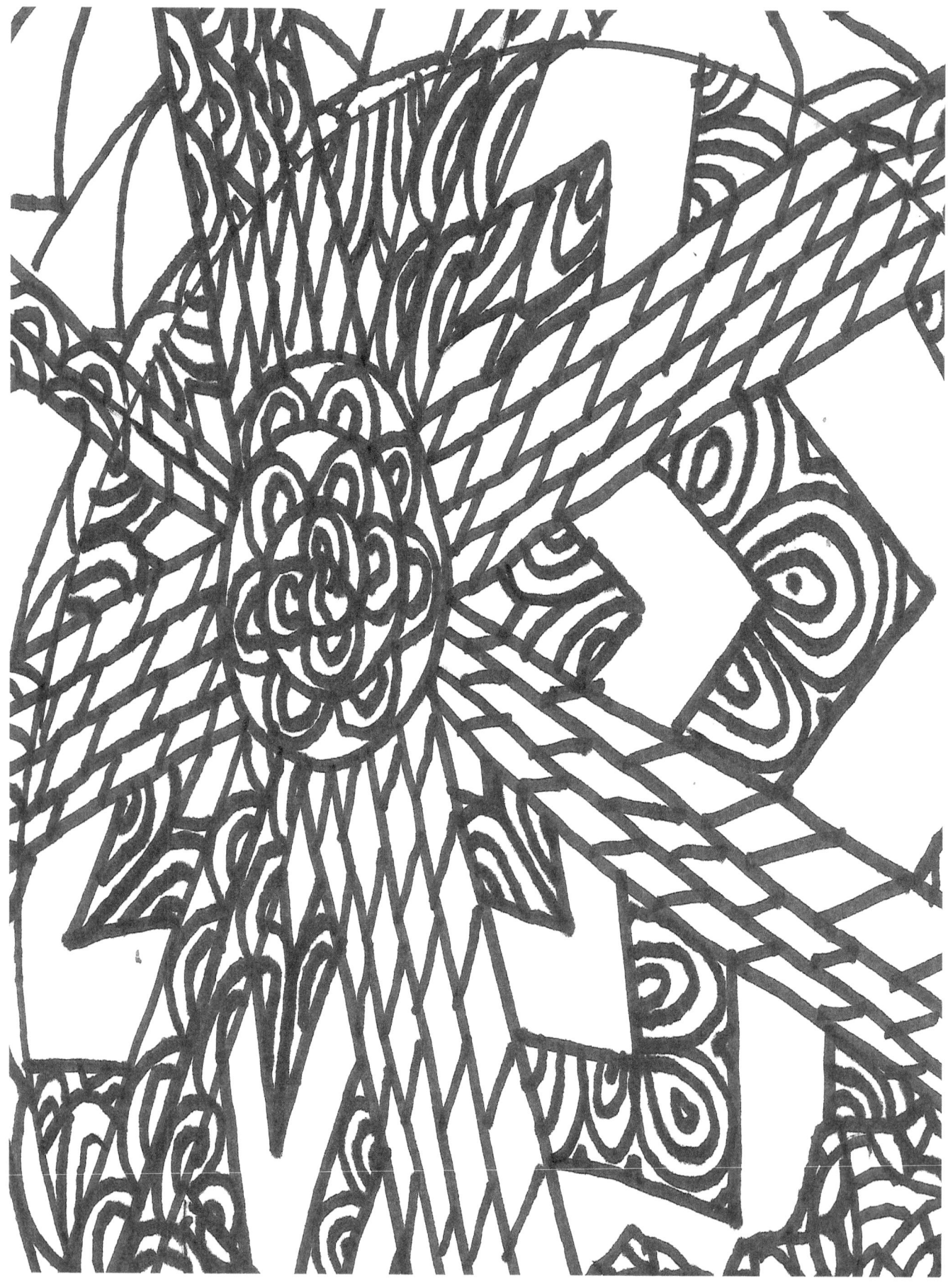

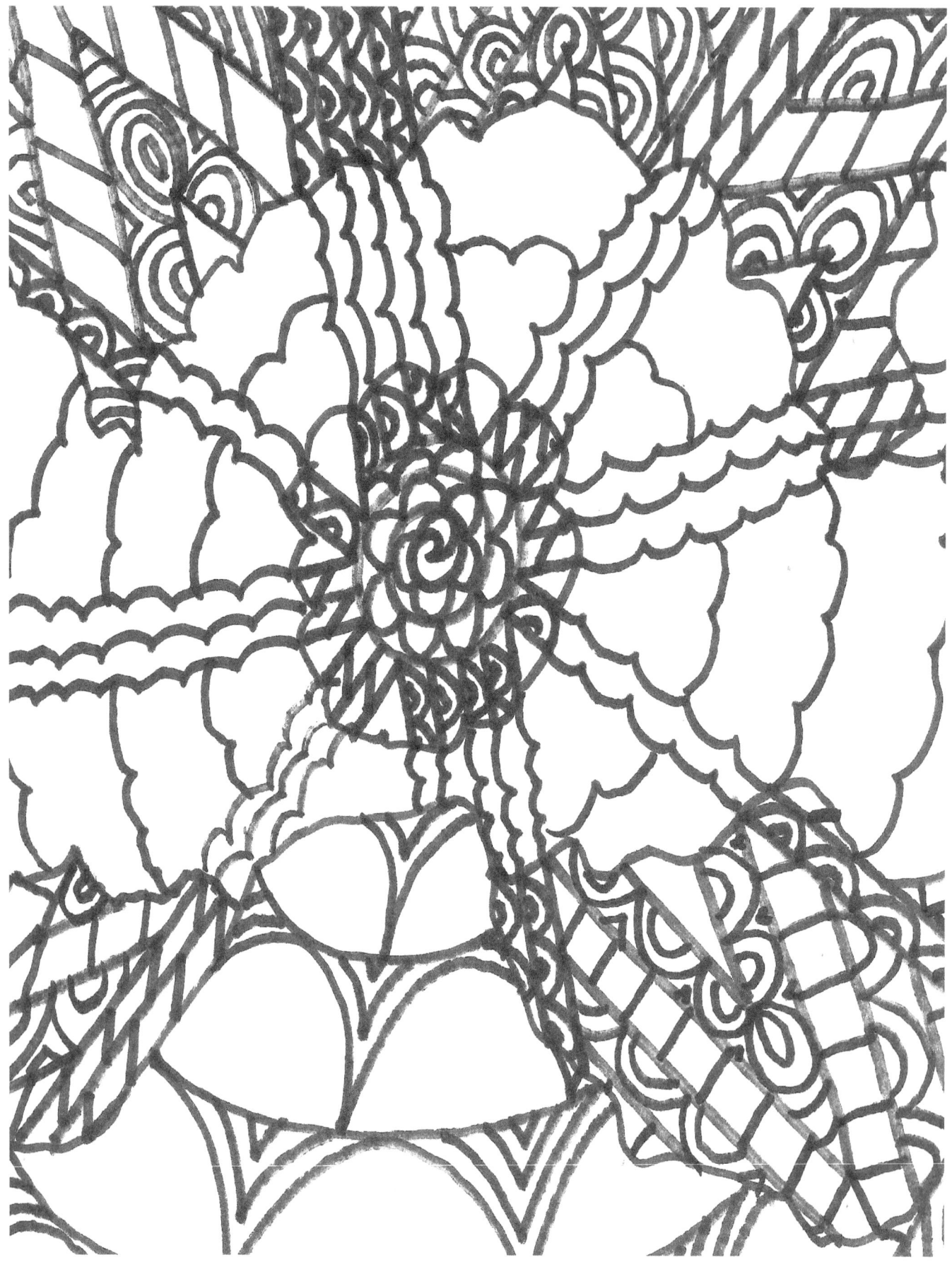

New Mexico Dreamscapes V

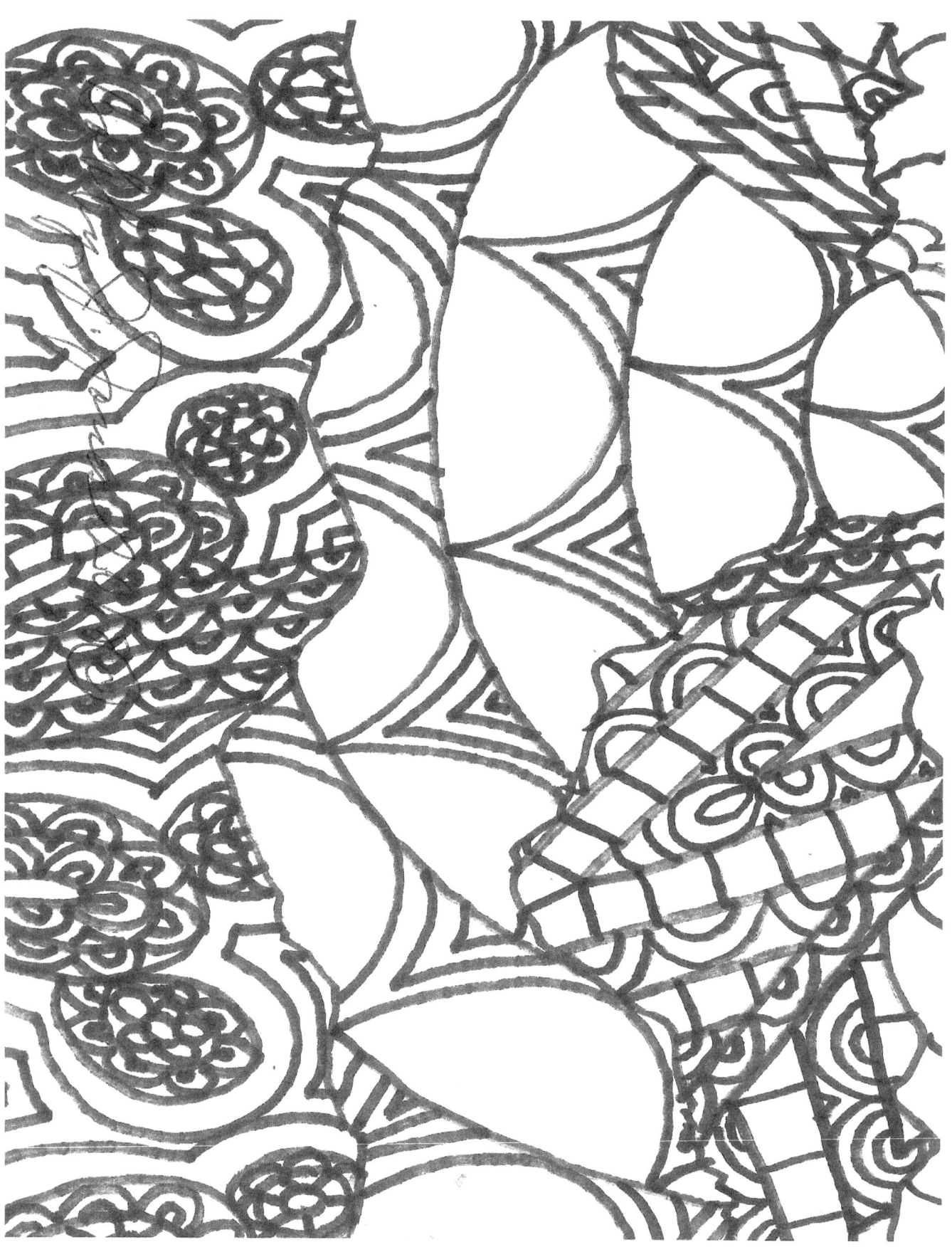

New Mexico Dreamscapes V

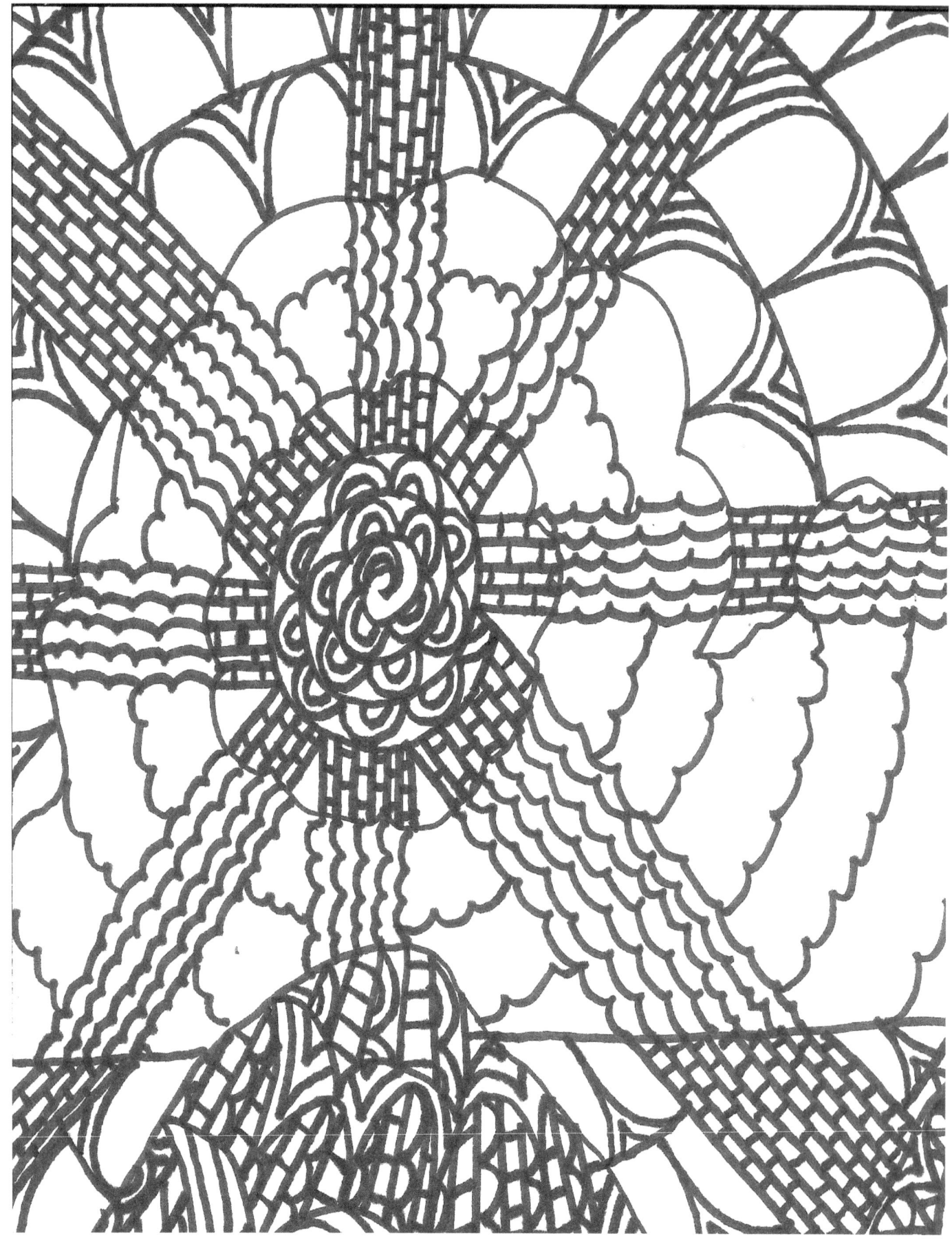

New Mexico Dreamscapes V

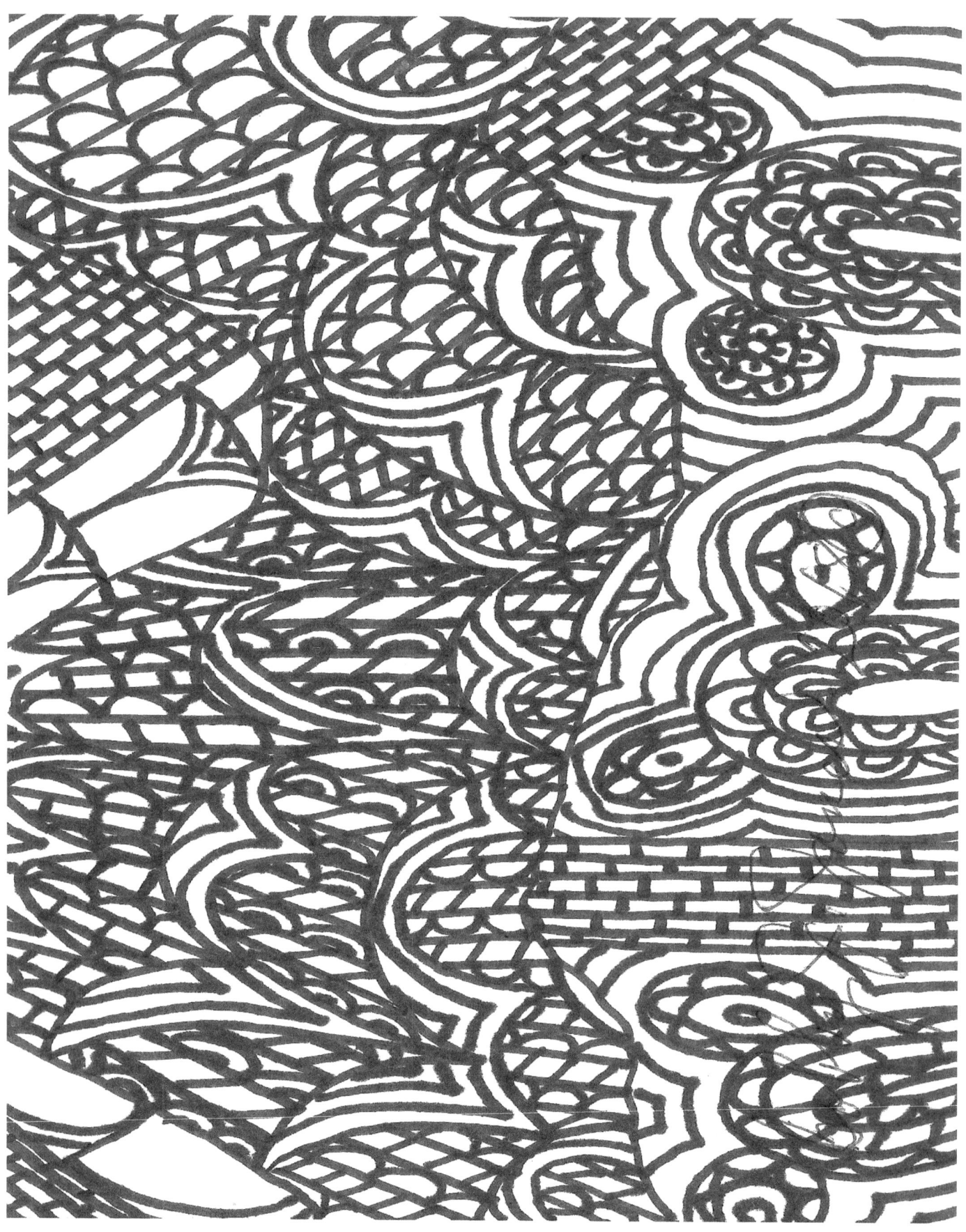

New Mexico Dreamscapes V

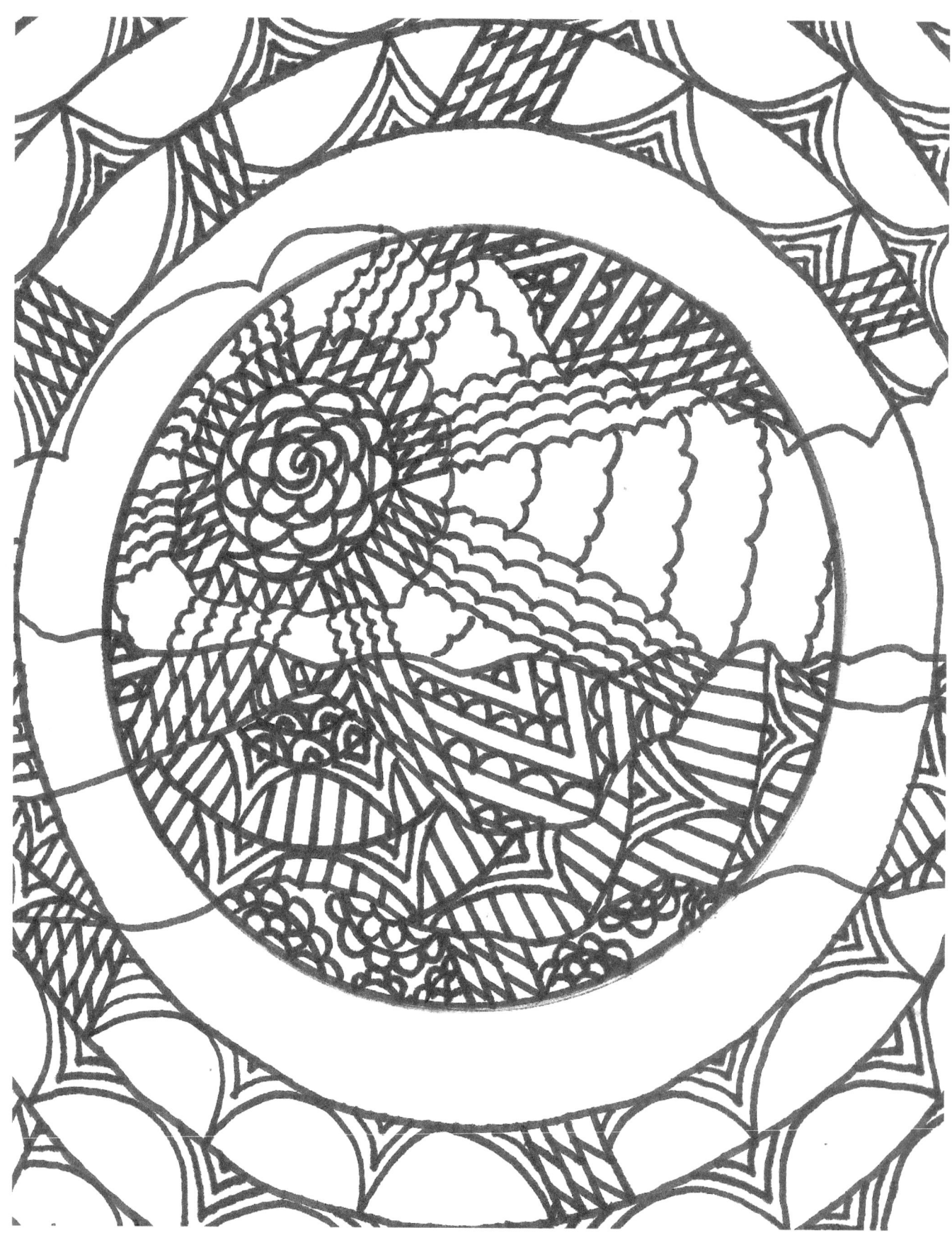

New Mexico Dreamscapes V

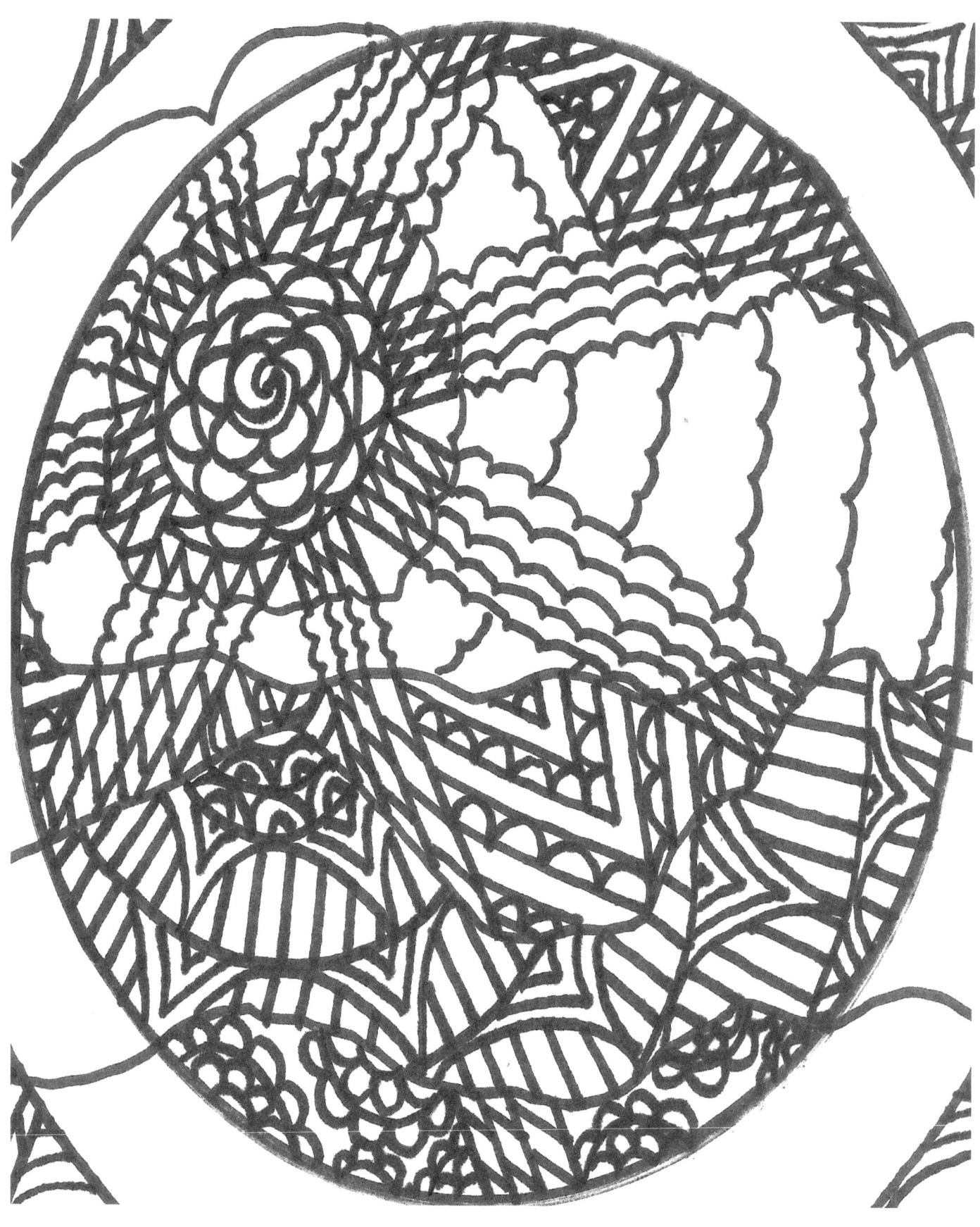

New Mexico Dreamscapes V

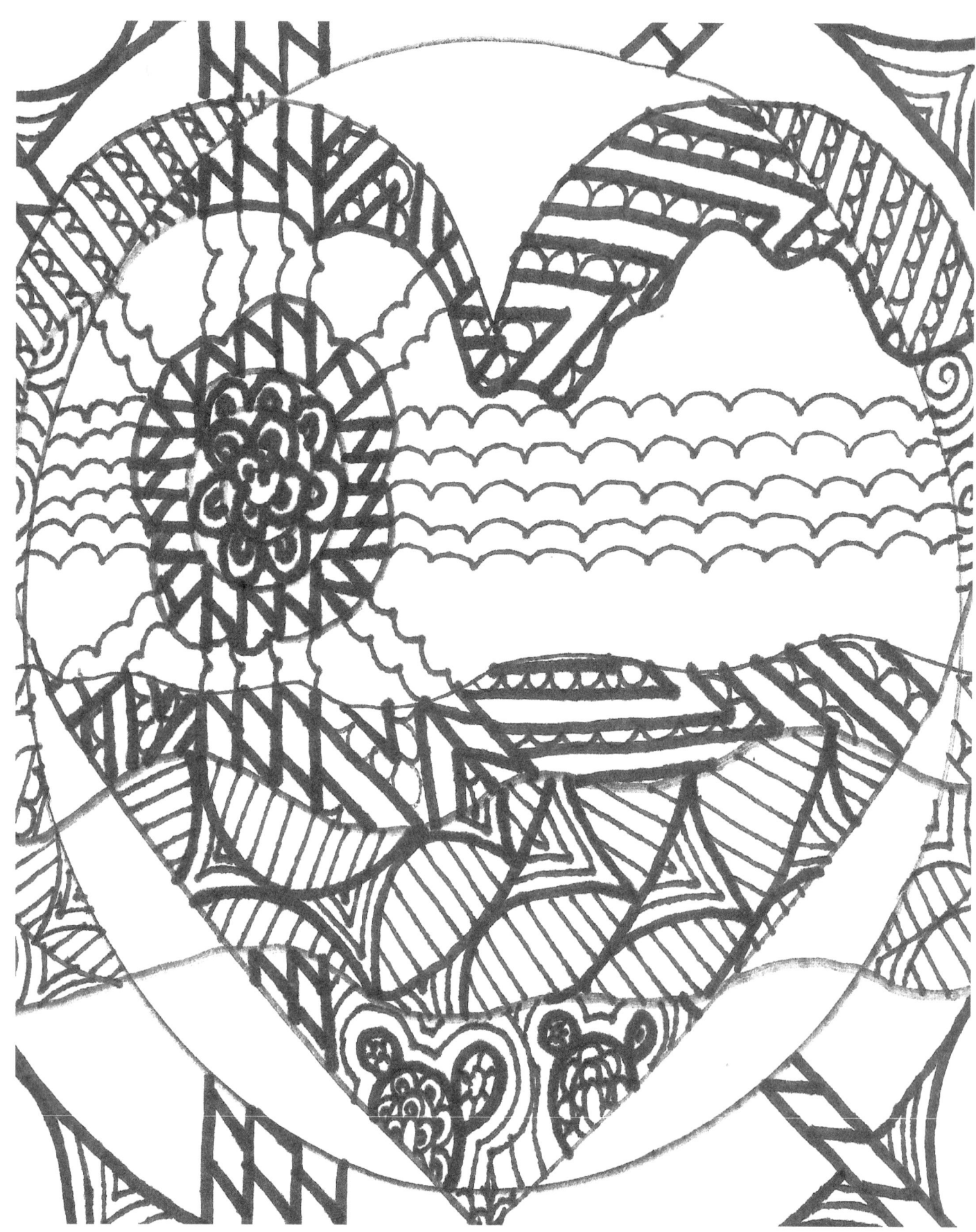

New Mexico Dreamscapes V

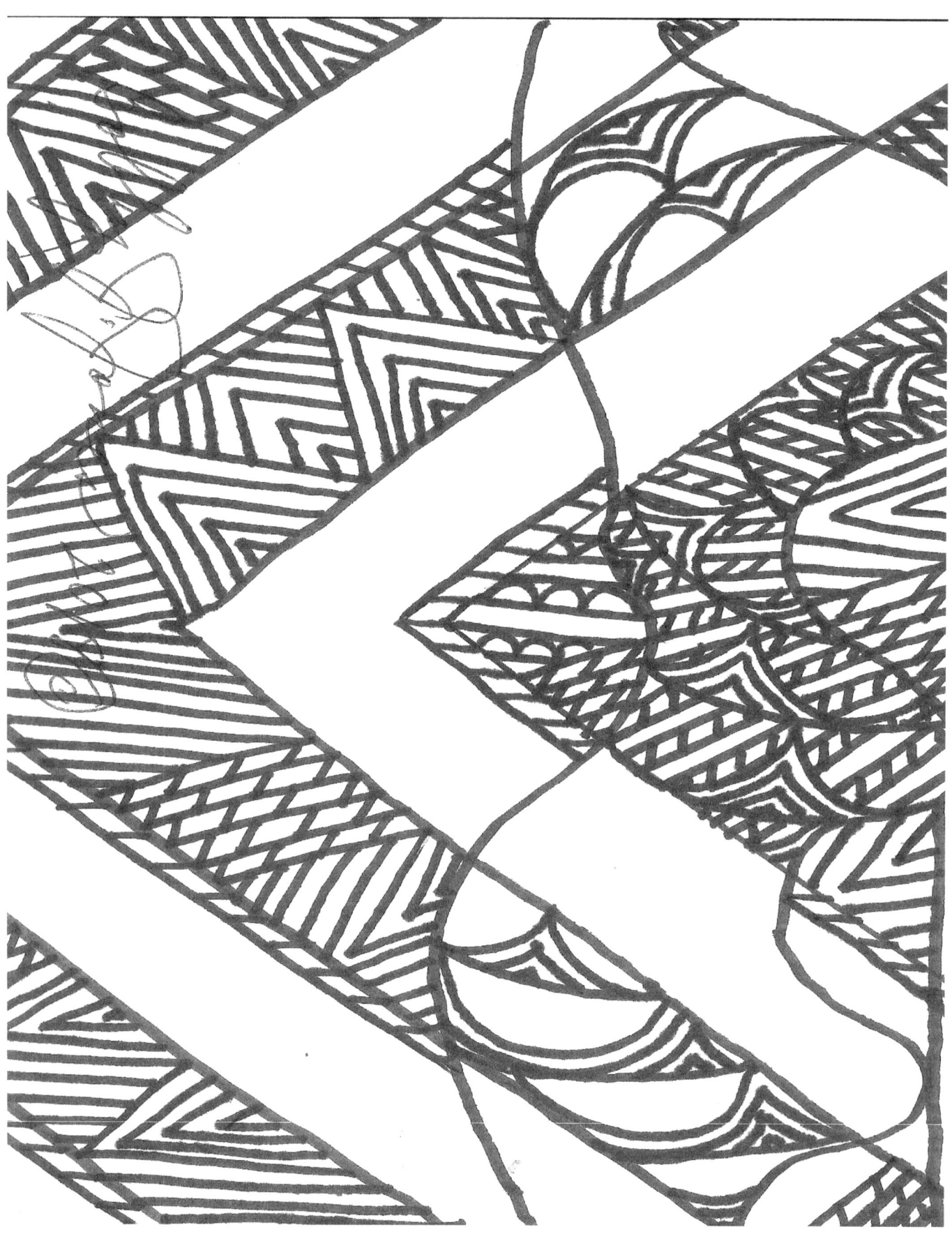

New Mexico Dreamscapes V

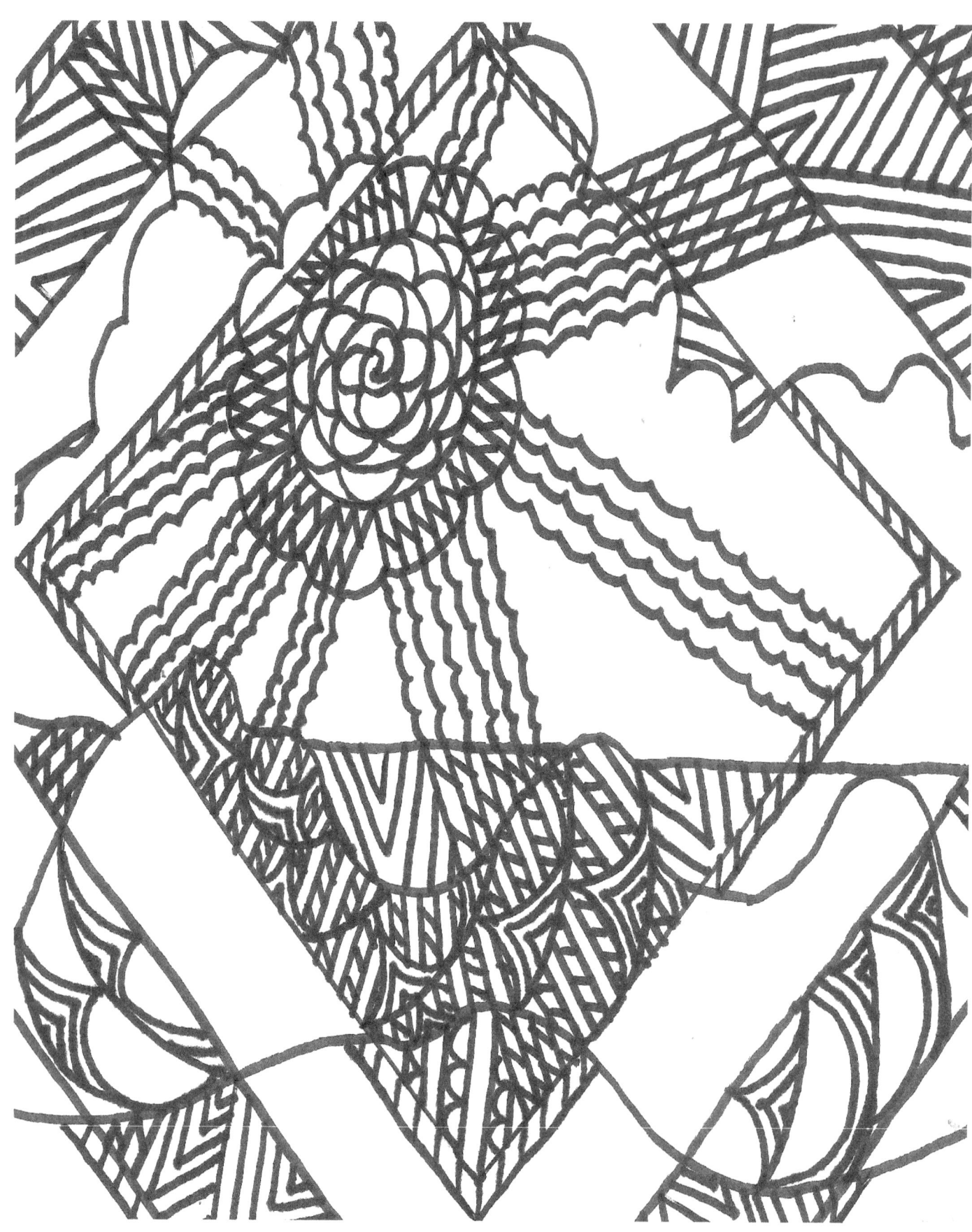

New Mexico Dreamscapes V

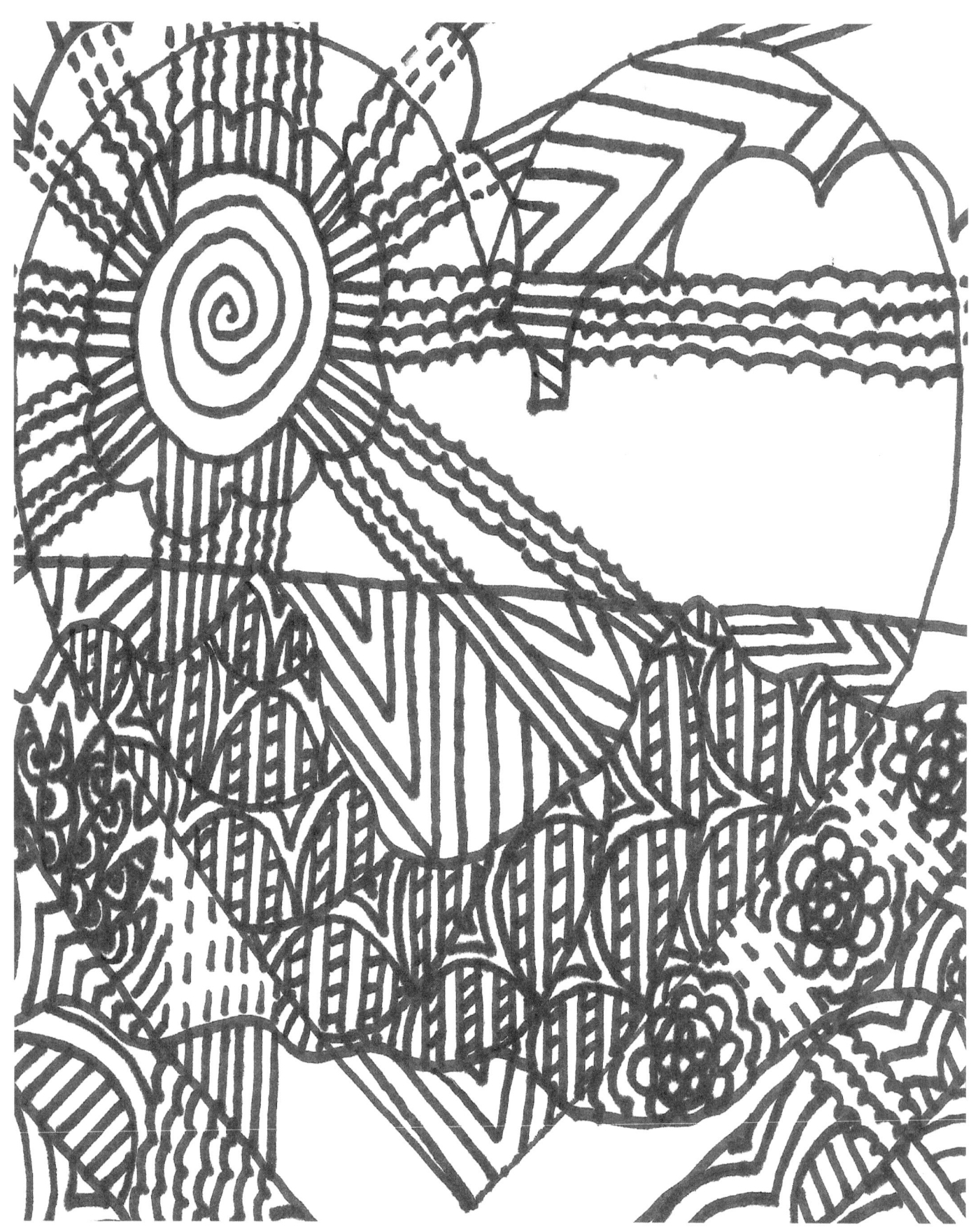

New Mexico Dreamscapes V

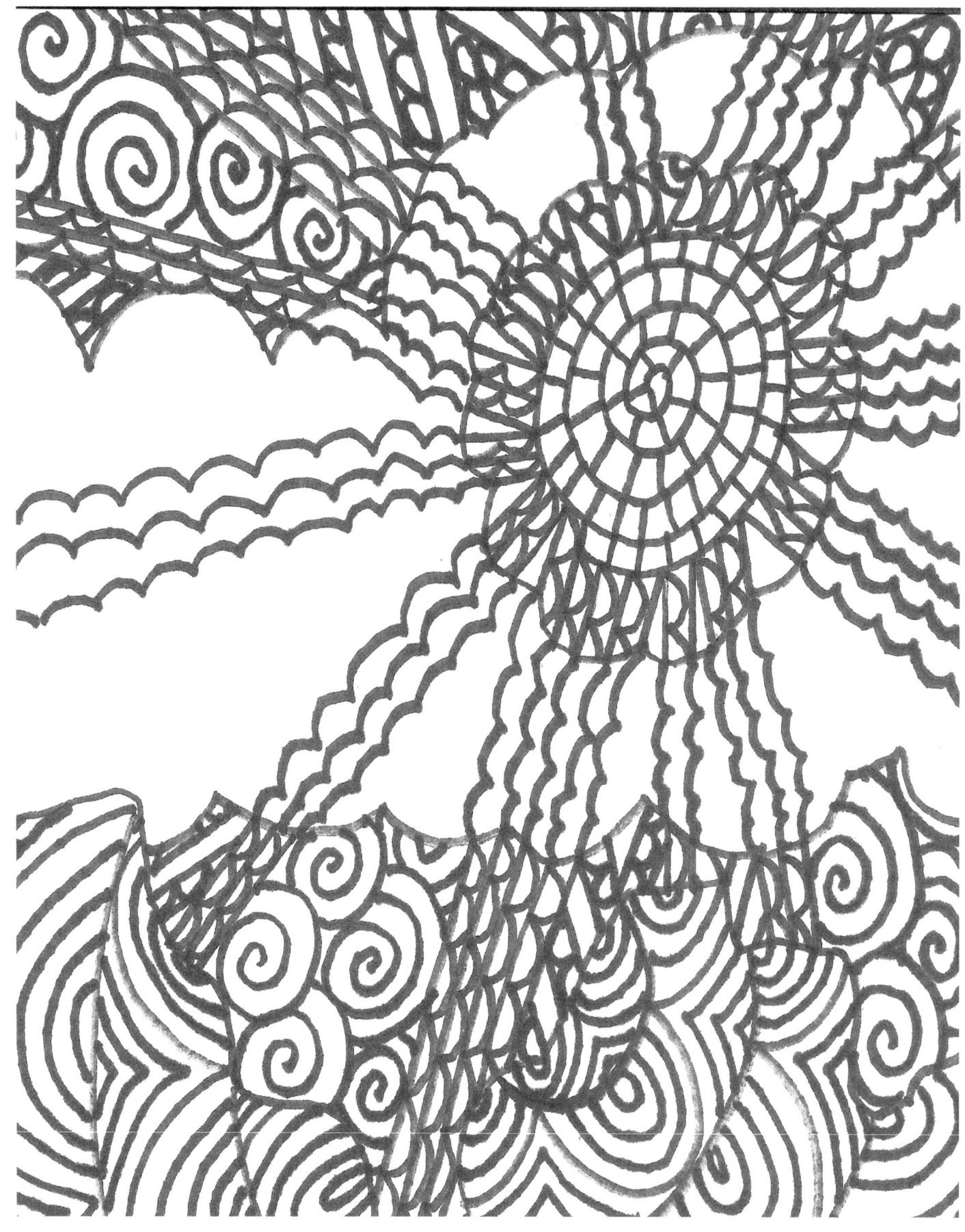

New Mexico Dreamscapes V

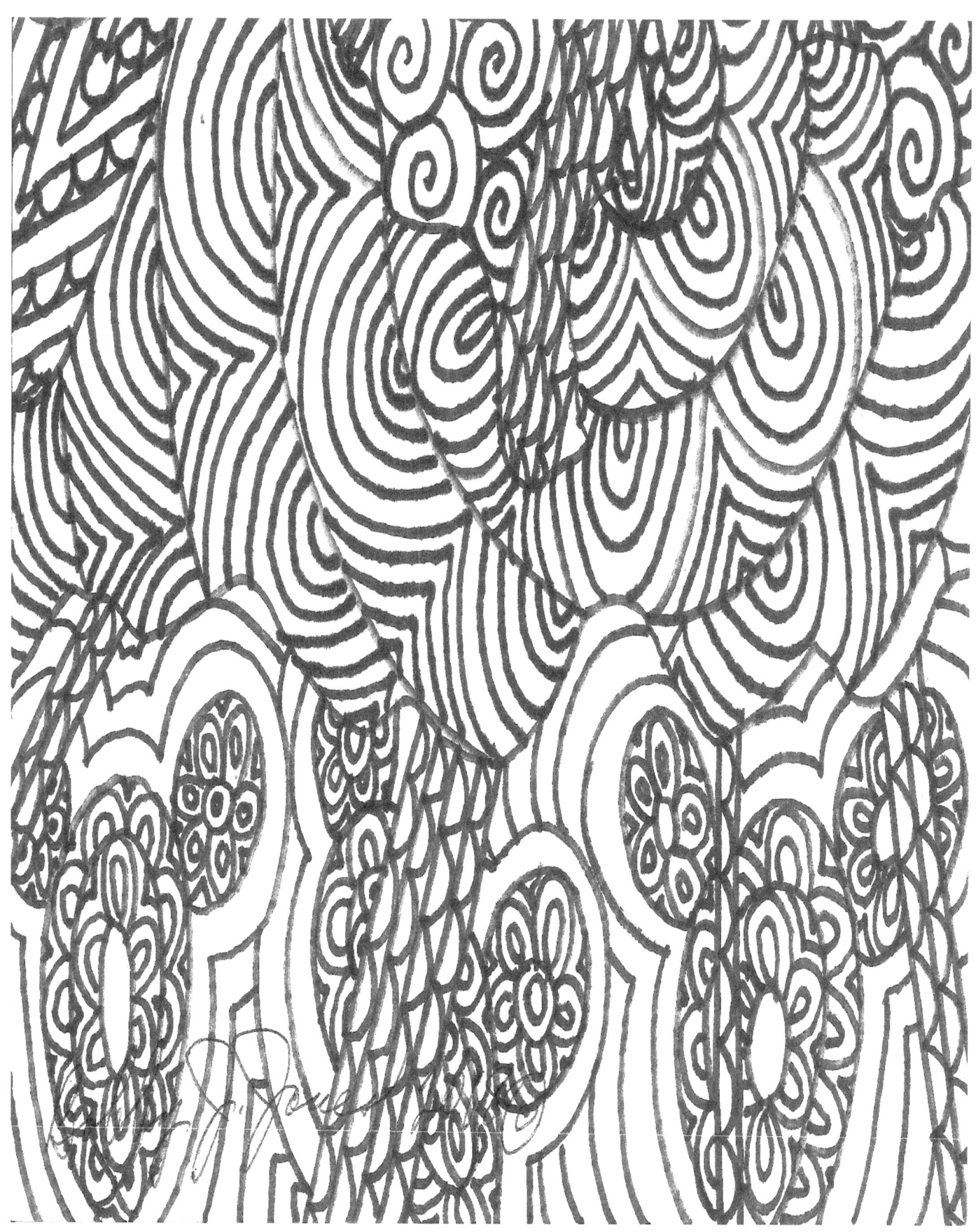

New Mexico Dreamscapes V

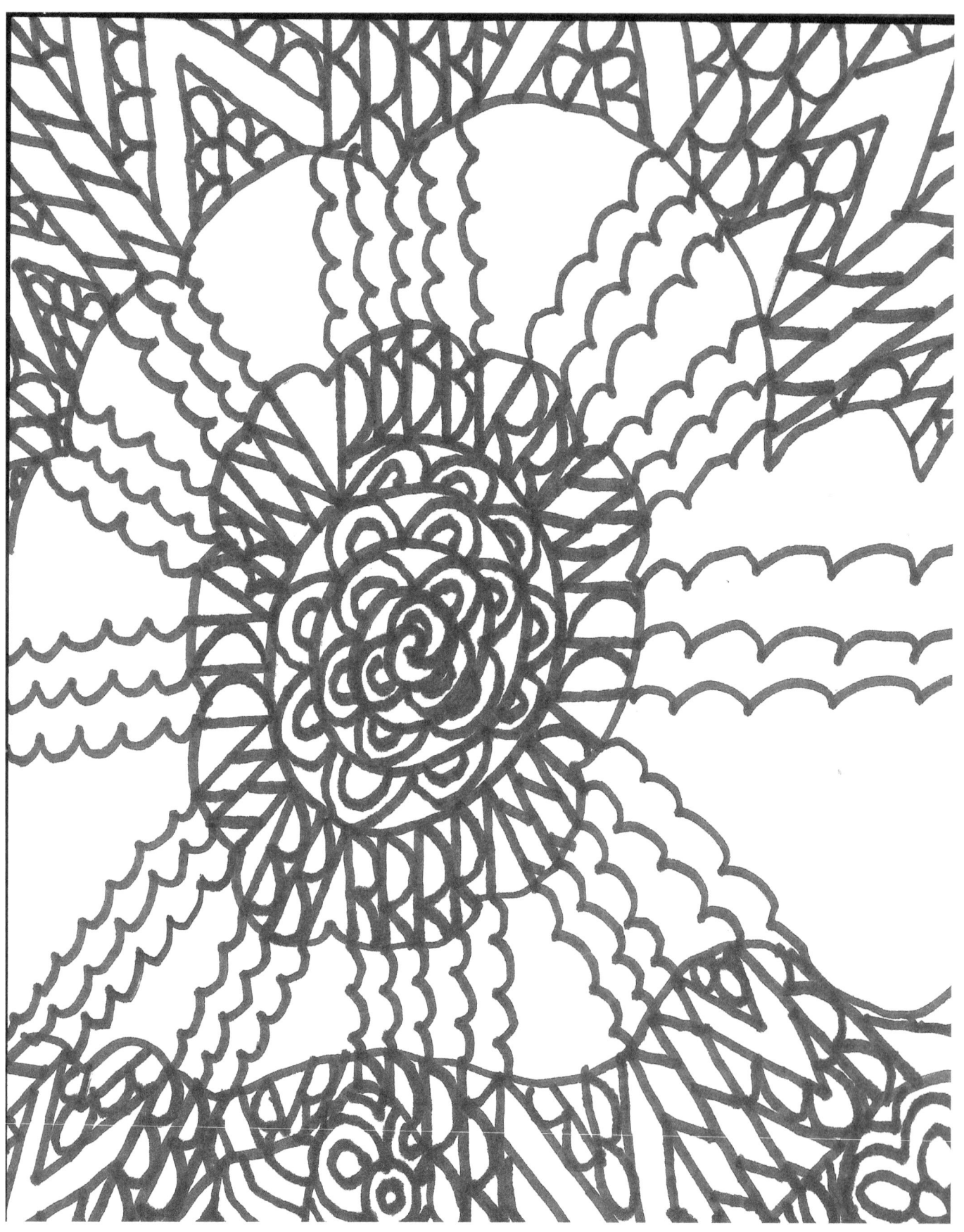

New Mexico Dreamscapes V

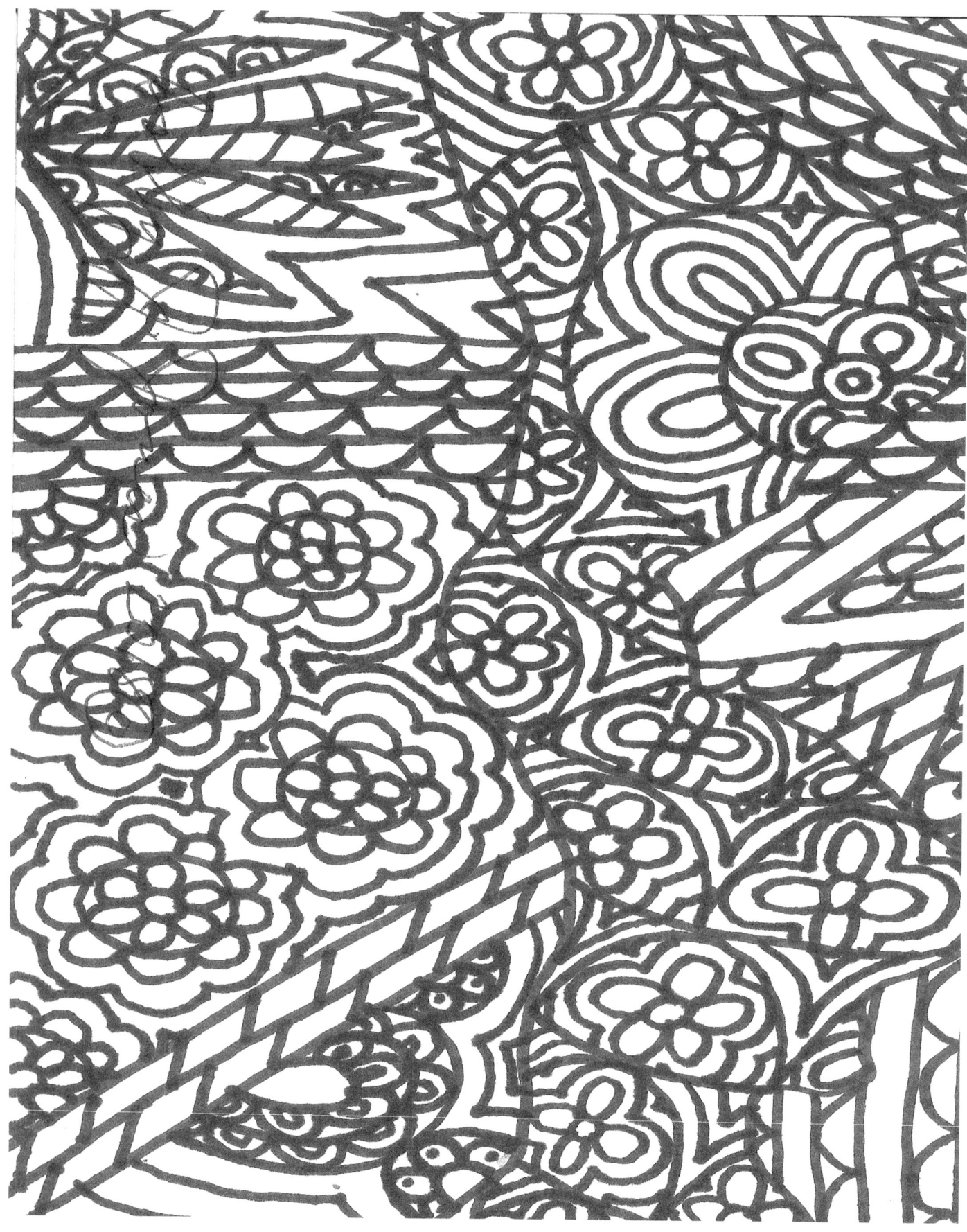

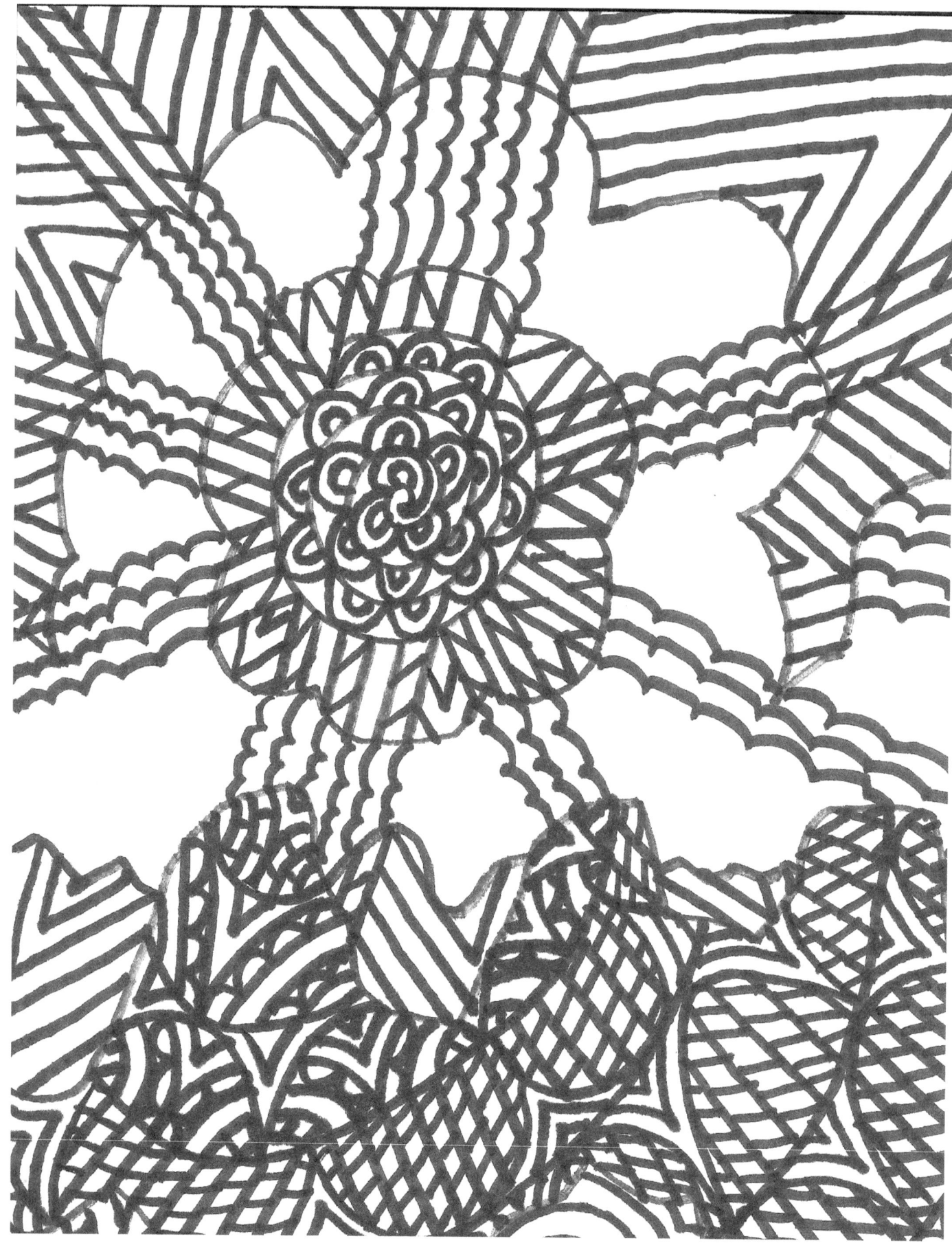

New Mexico Dreamscapes V

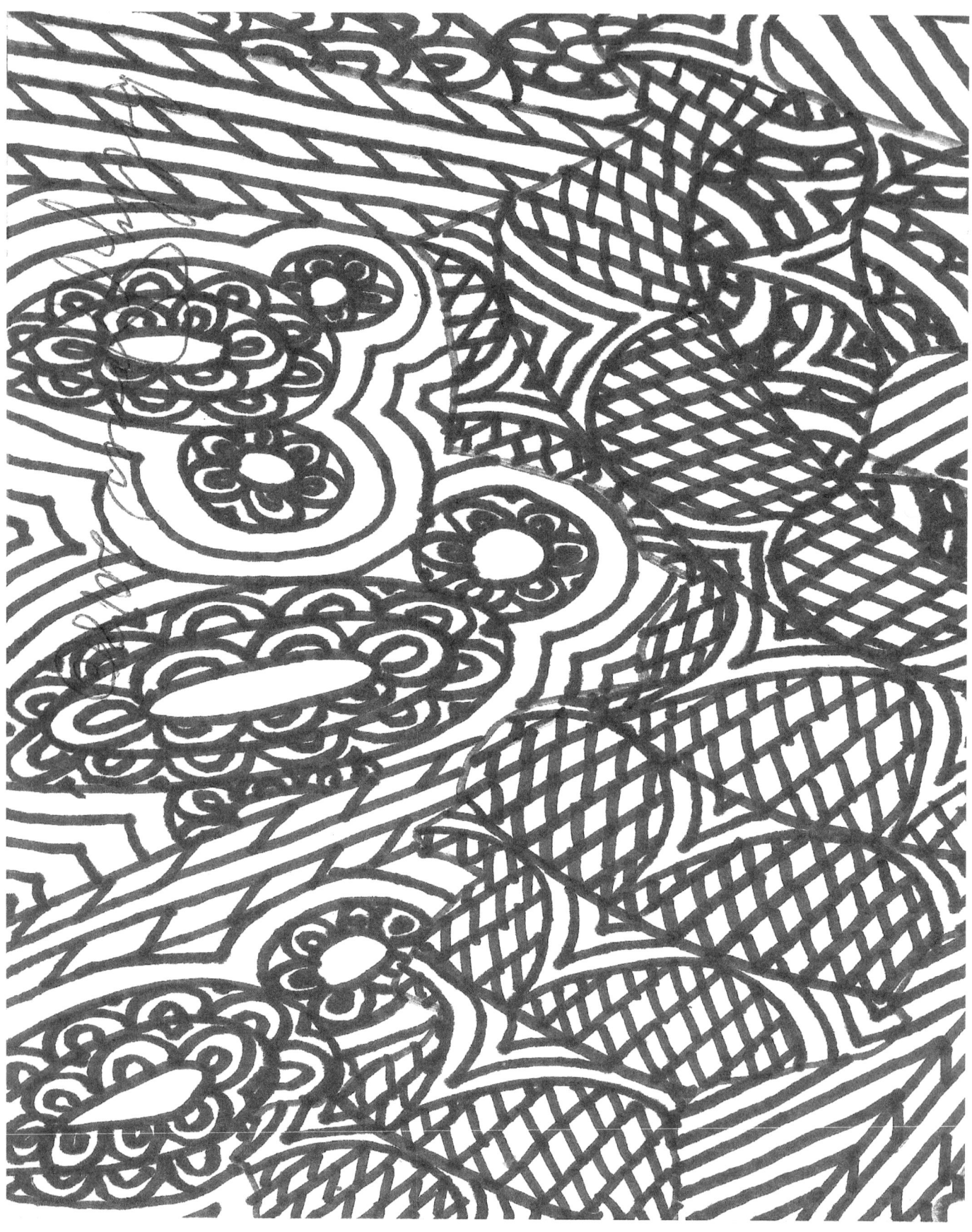

New Mexico Dreamscapes V

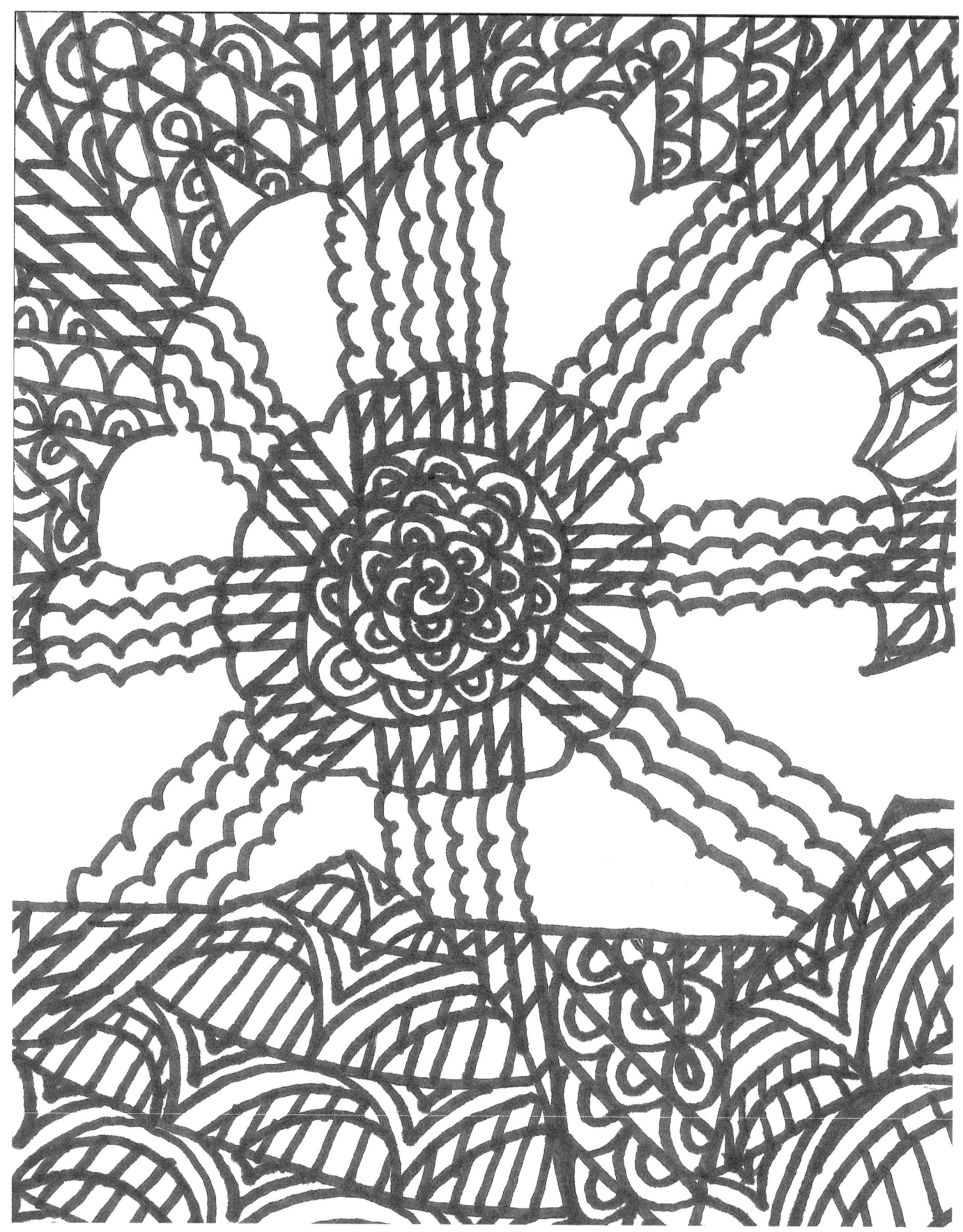

New Mexico Dreamscapes V

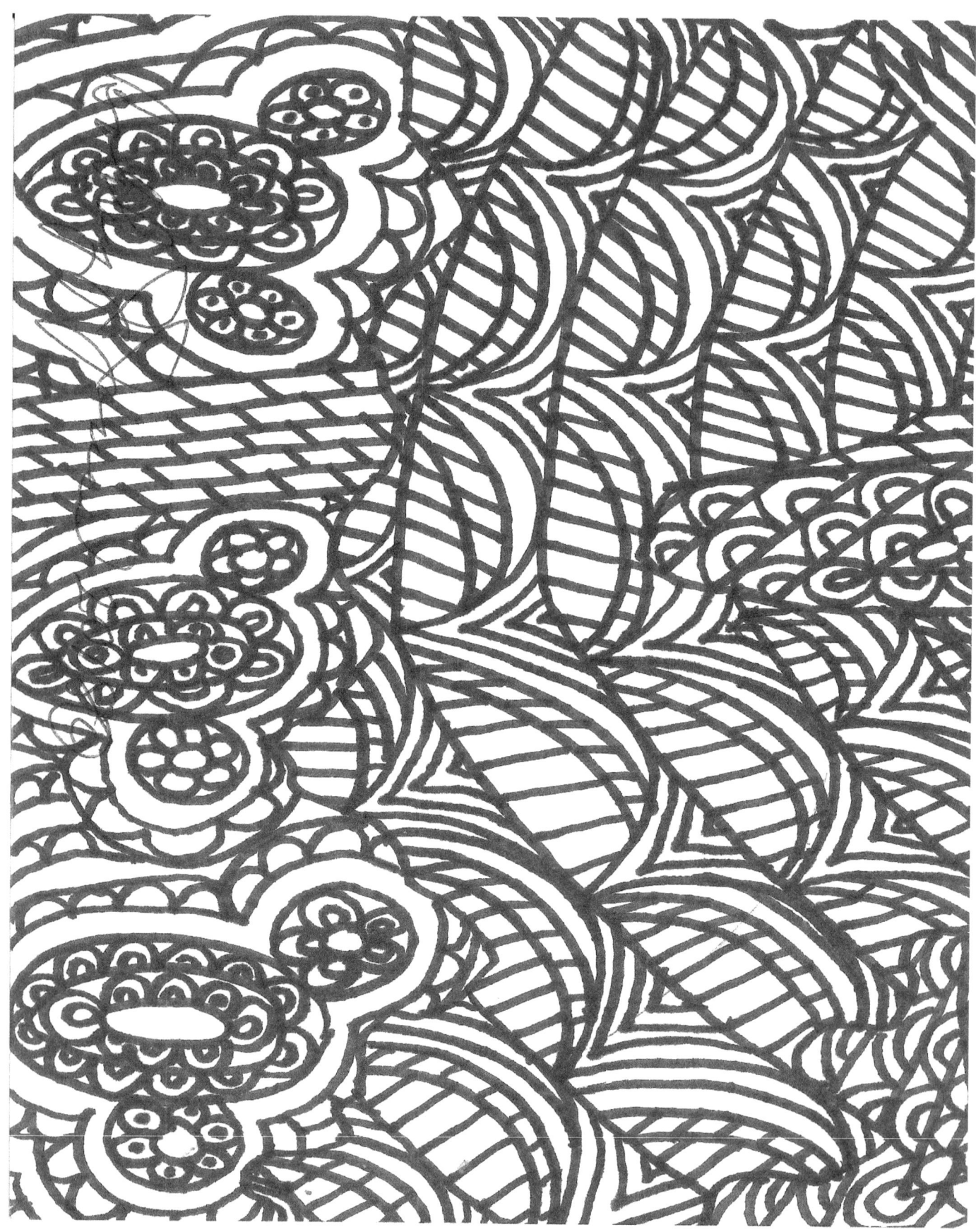

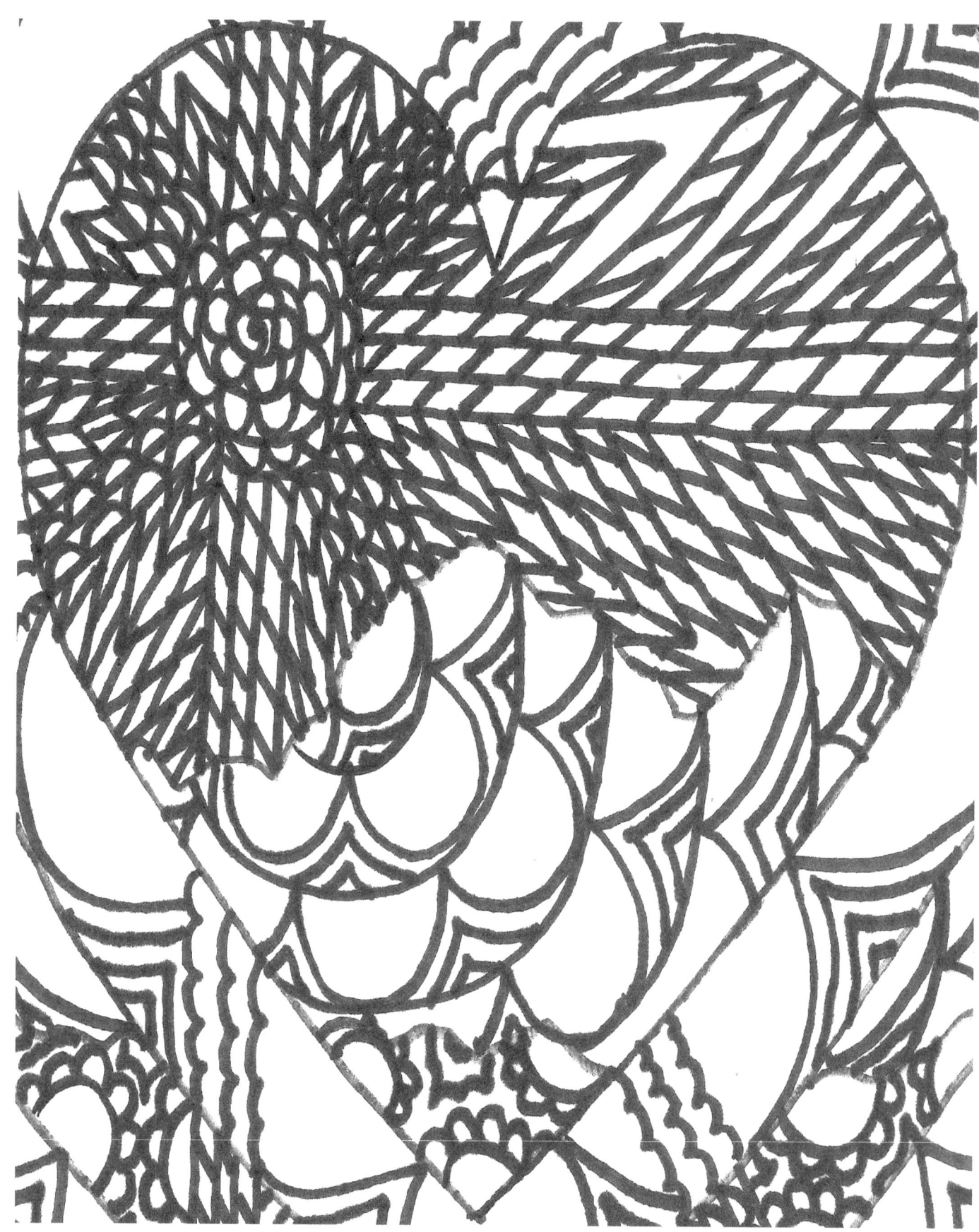

New Mexico Dreamscapes V

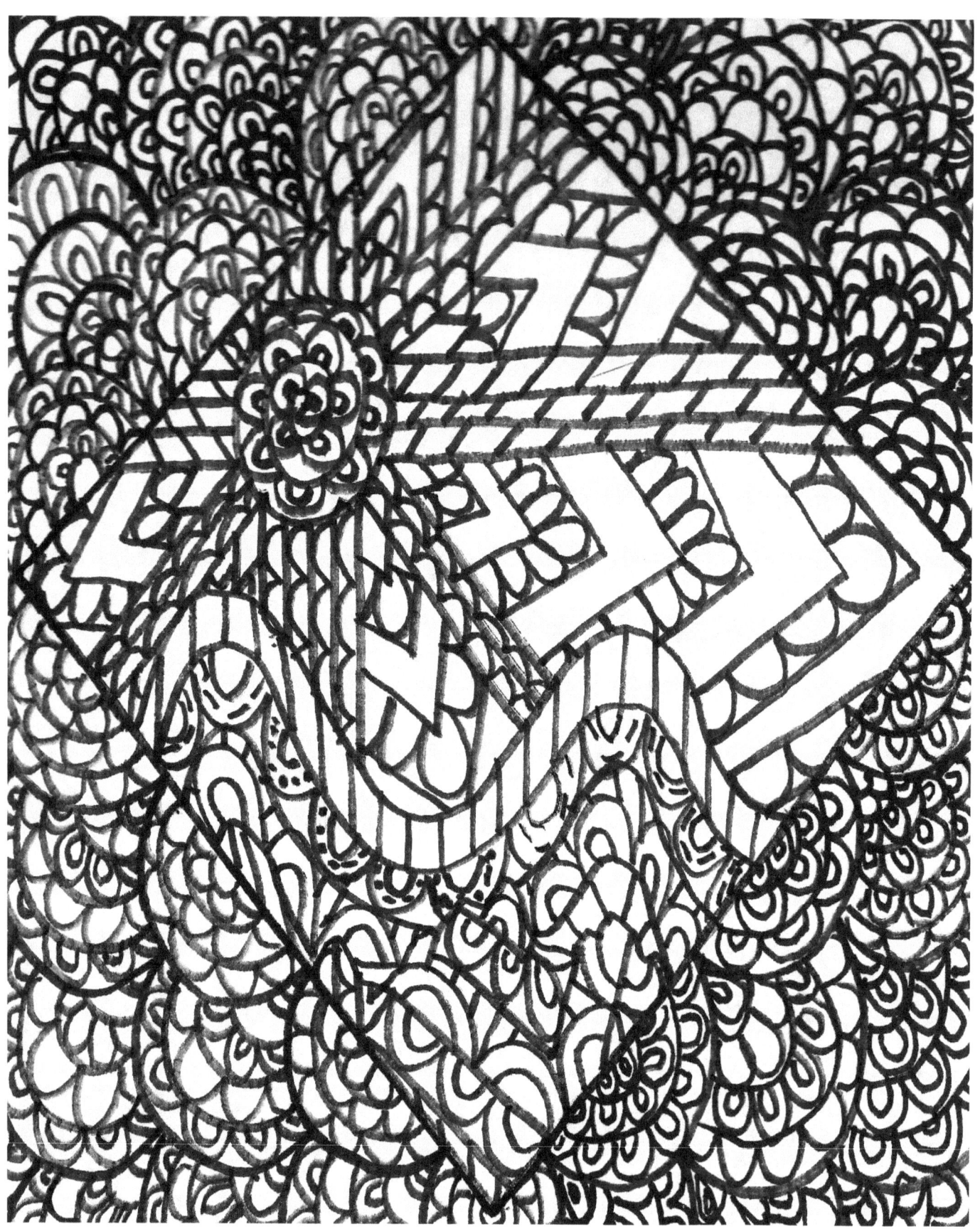

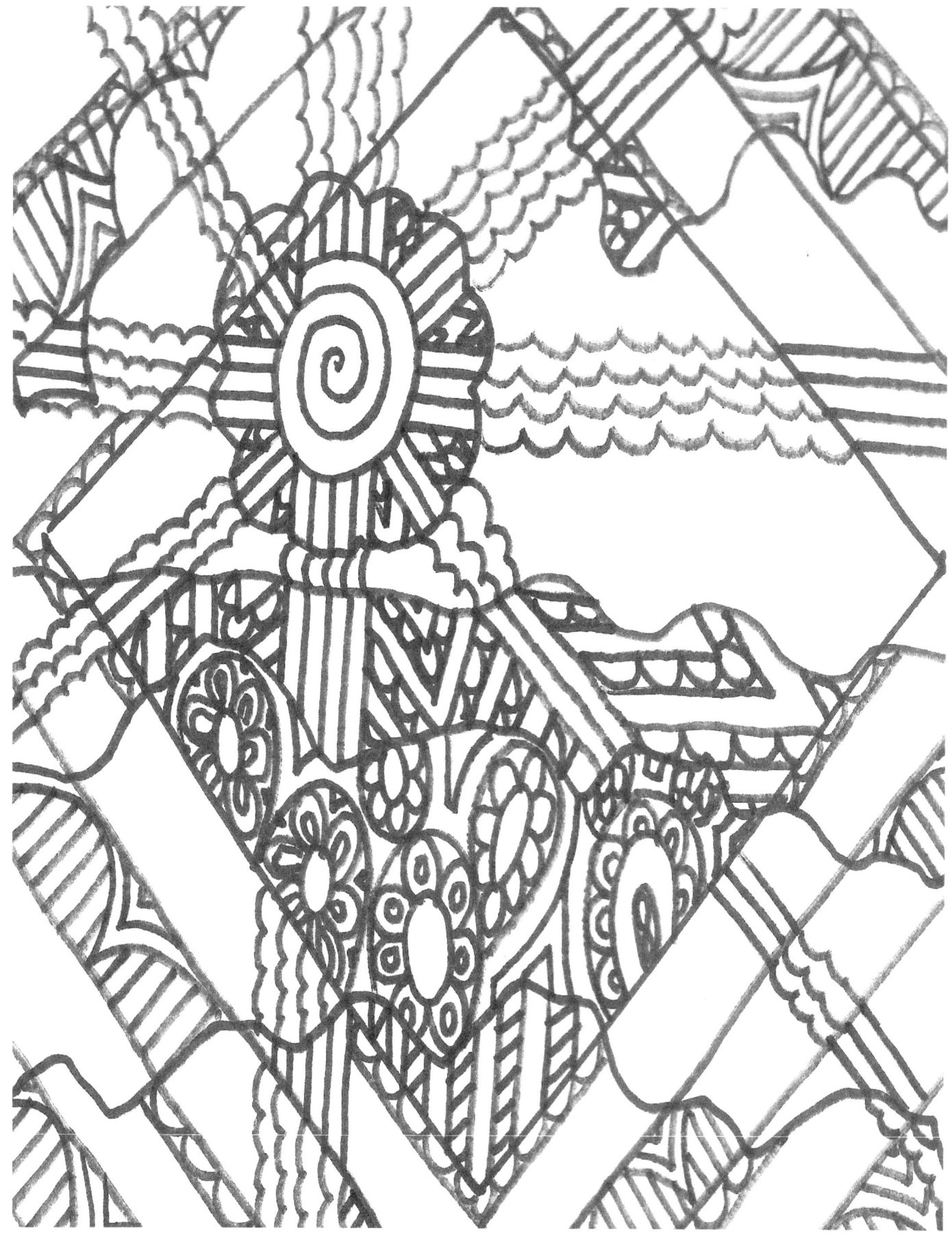

New Mexico Dreamscapes V

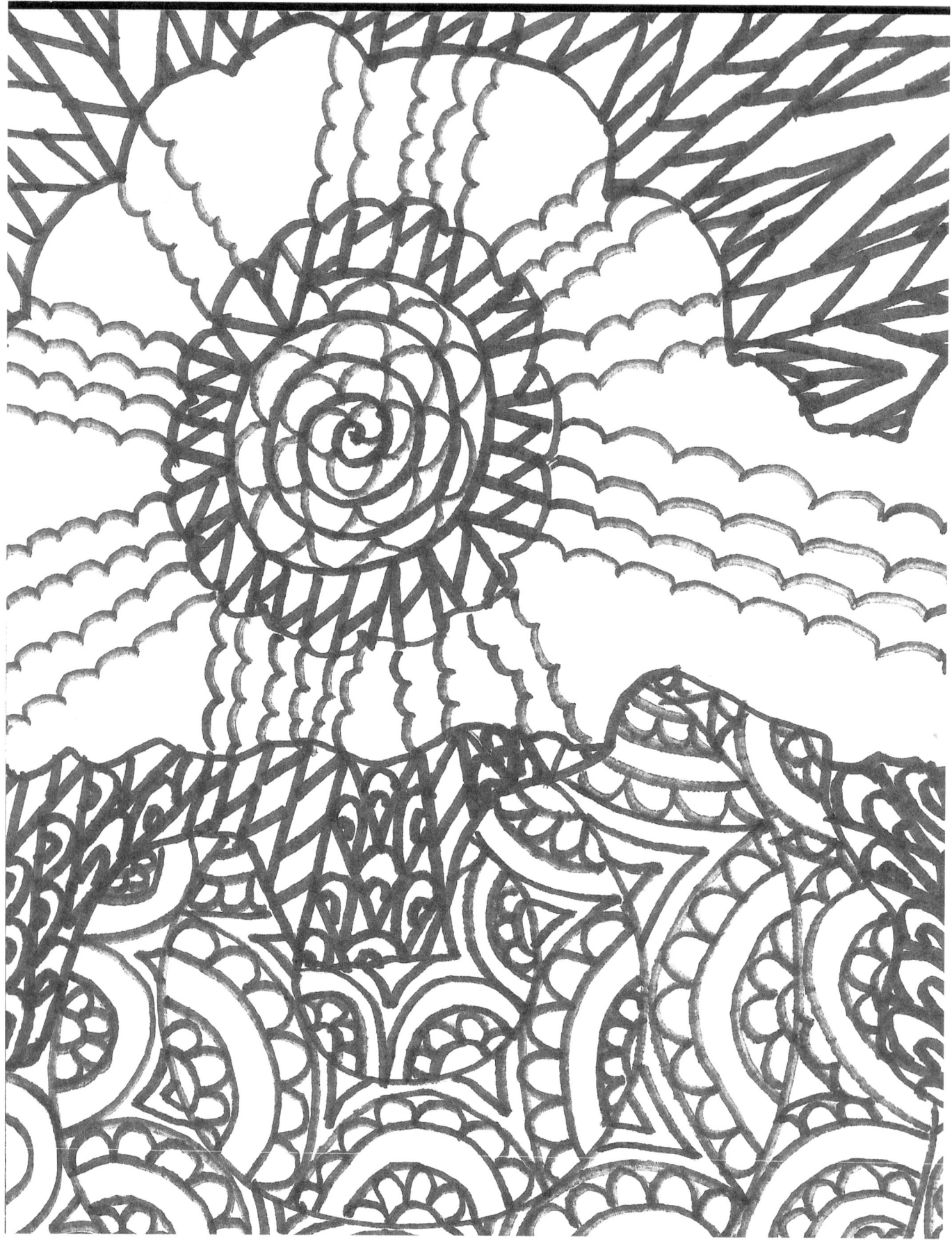

New Mexico Dreamscapes V

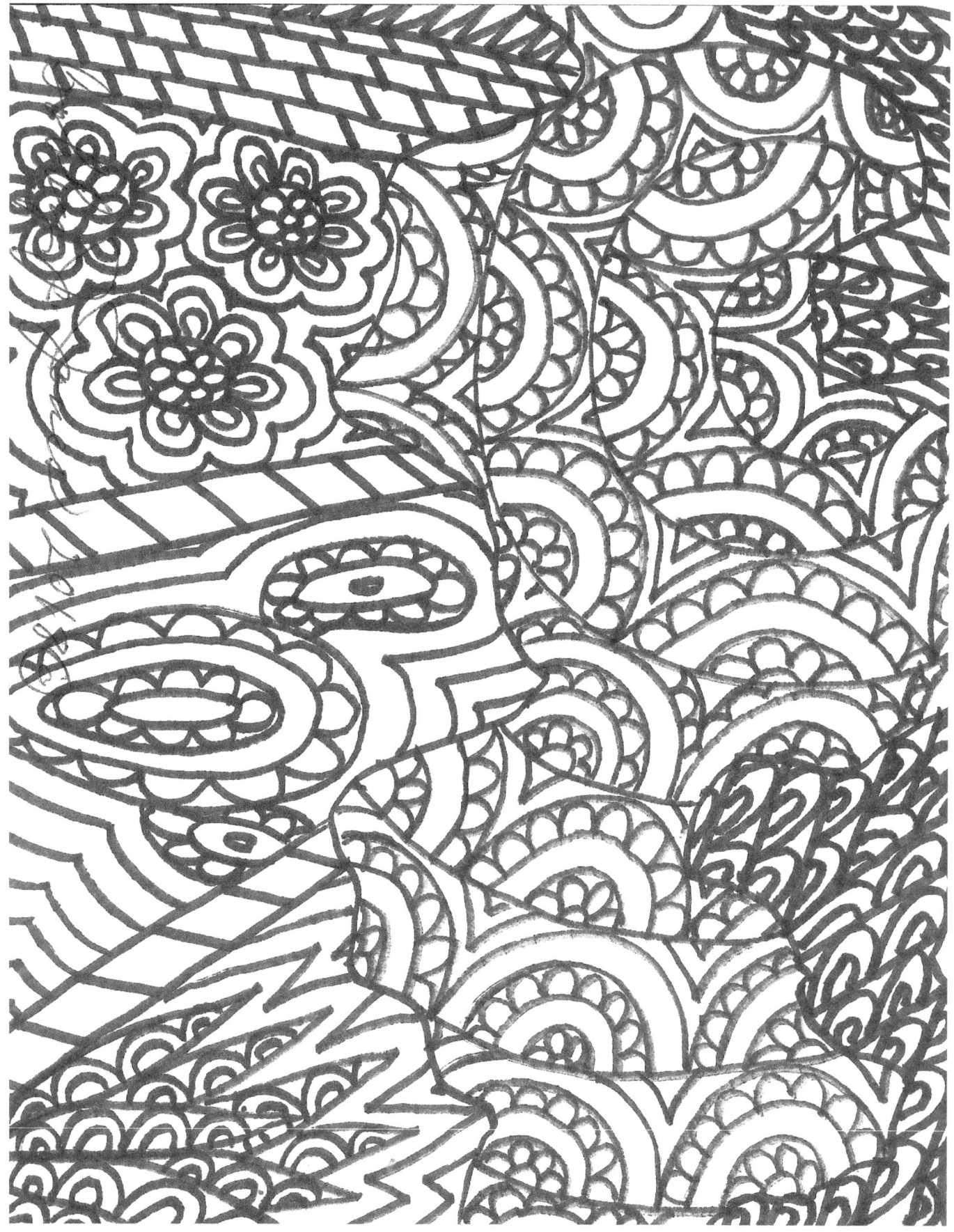

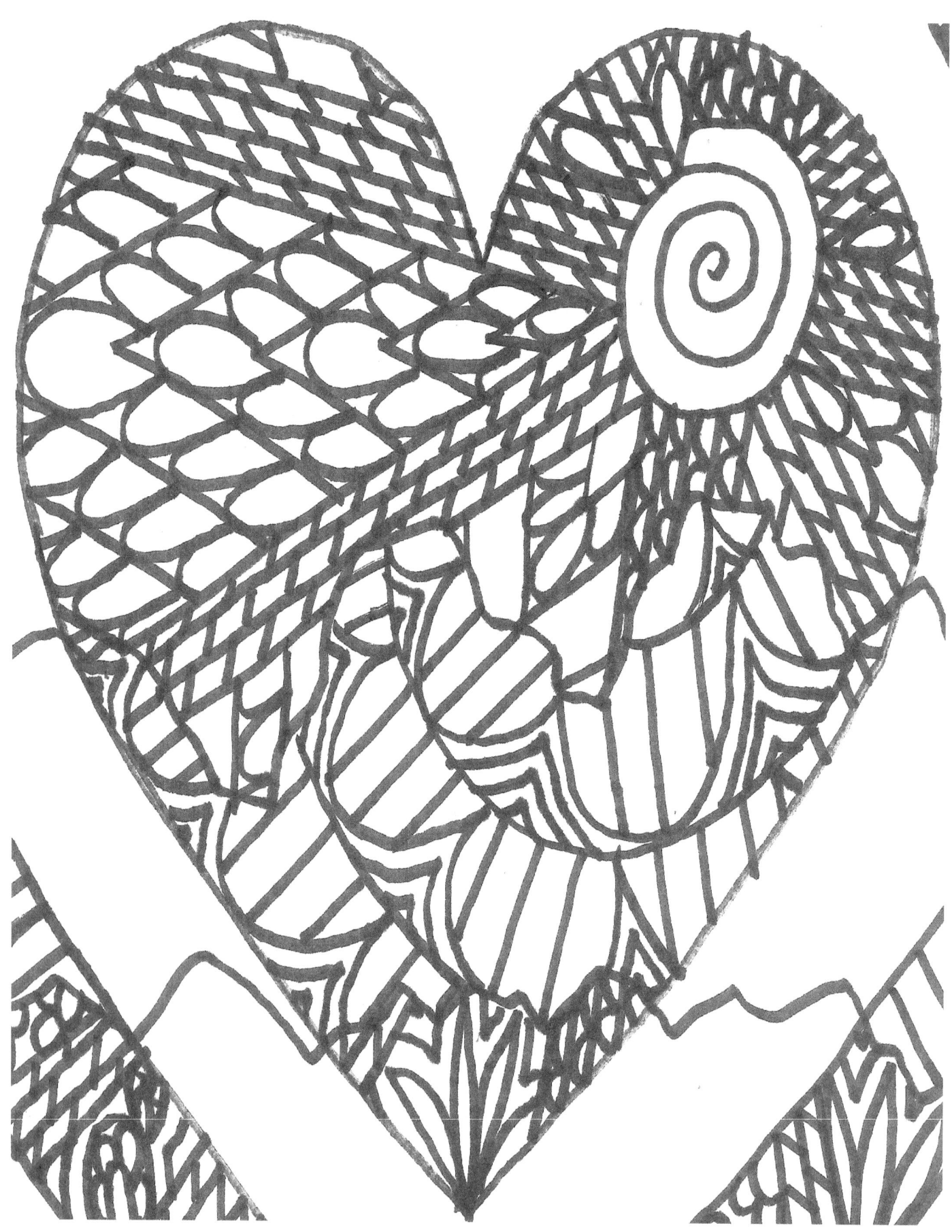

New Mexico Dreamscapes V

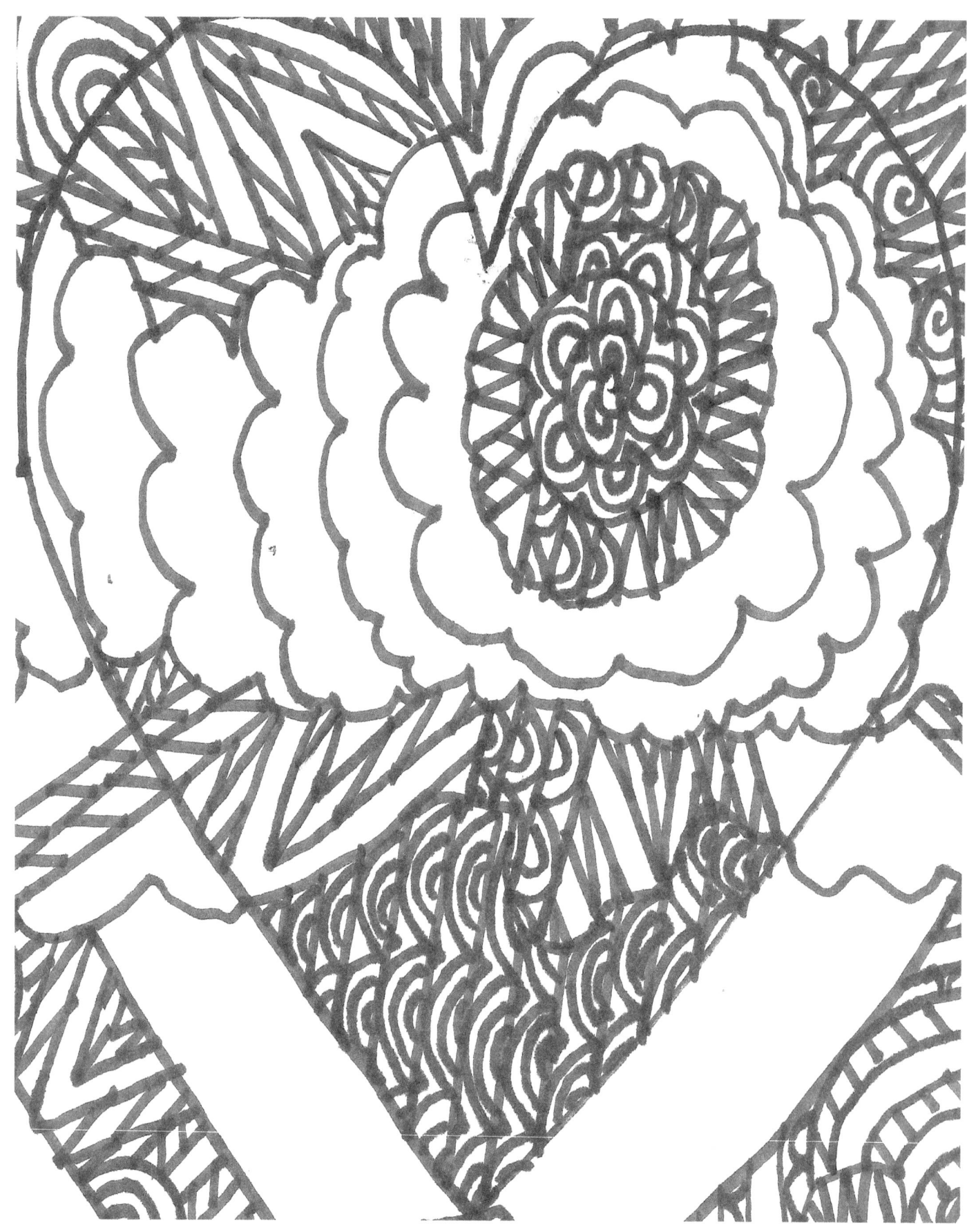

New Mexico Dreamscapes V

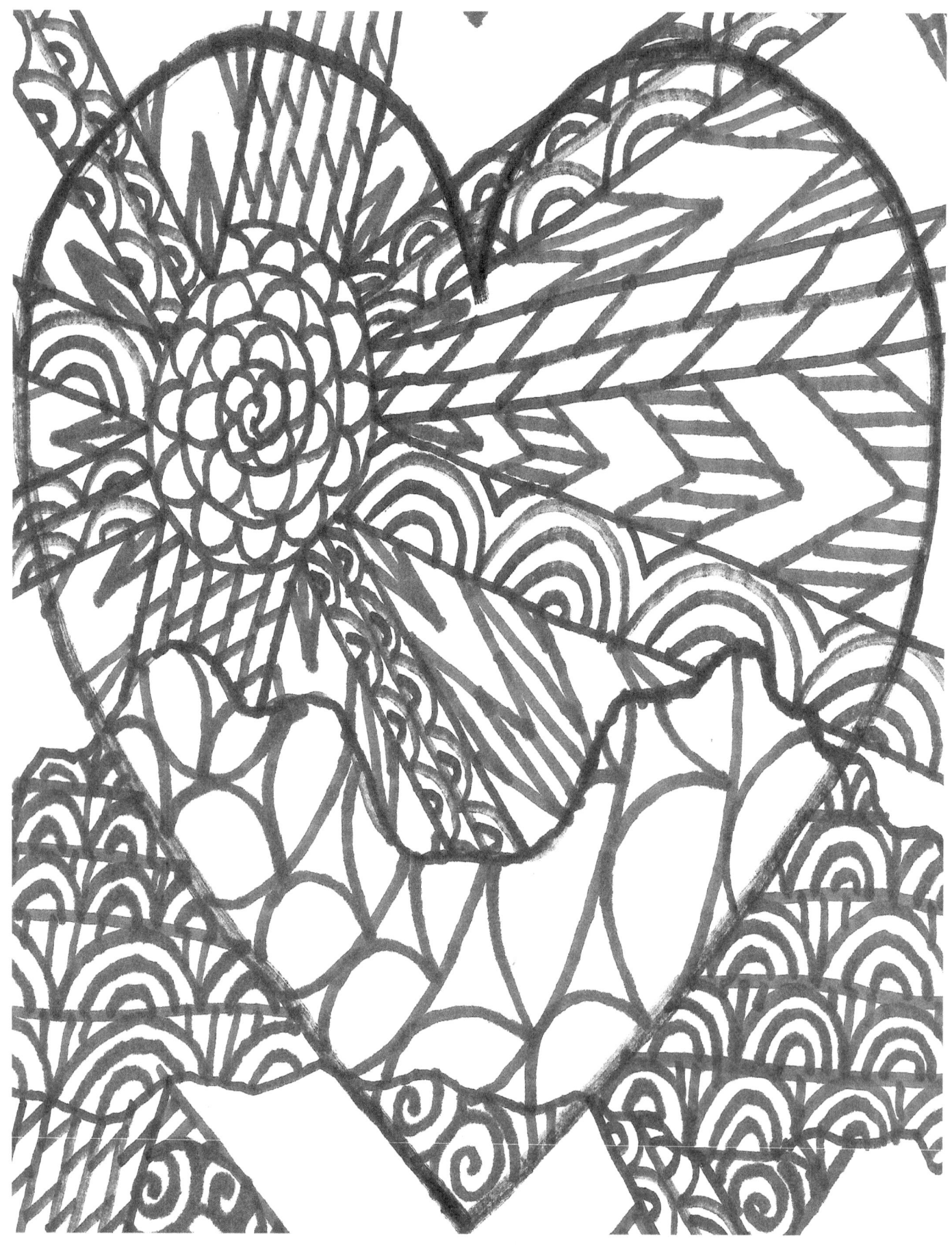

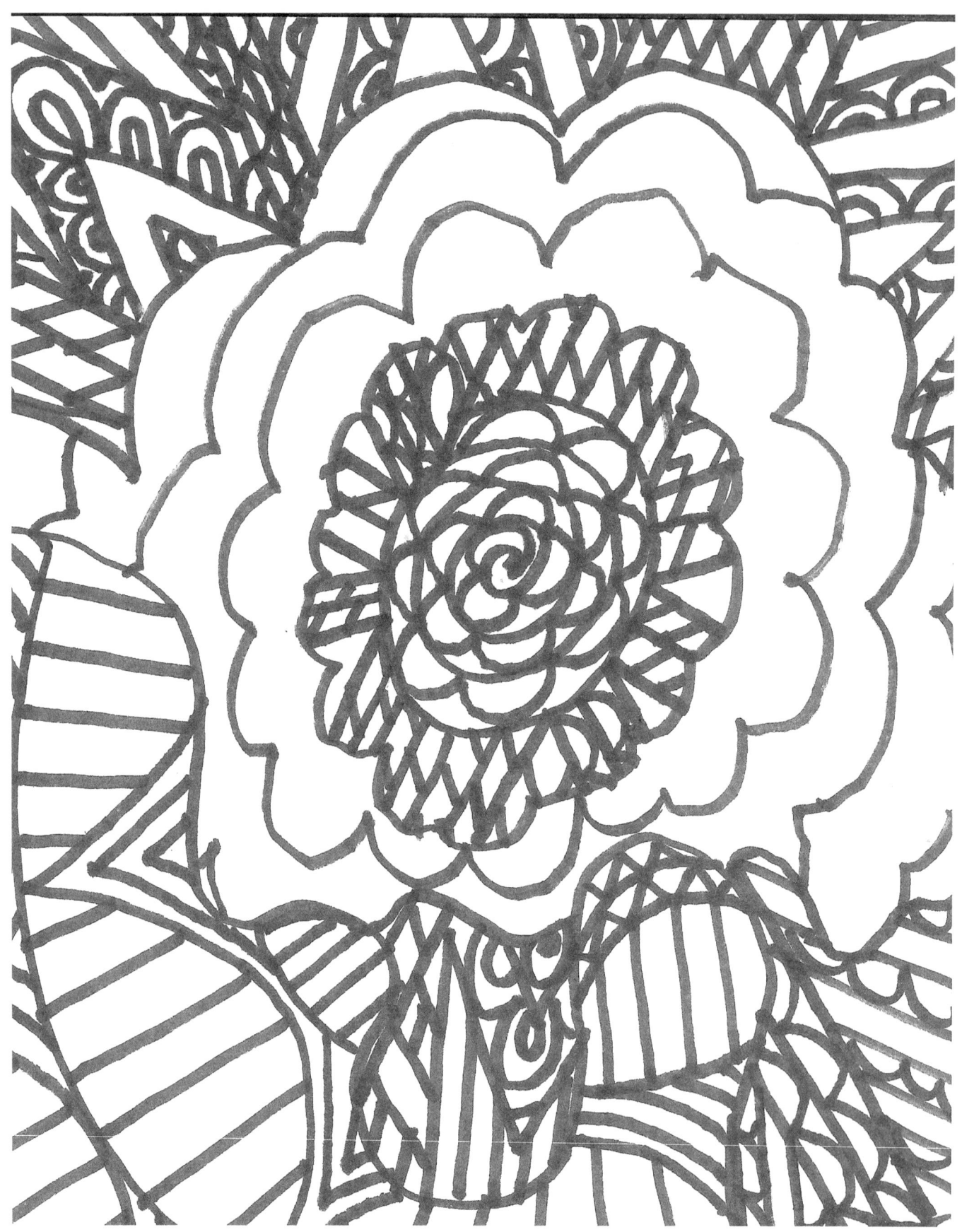

New Mexico Dreamscapes V

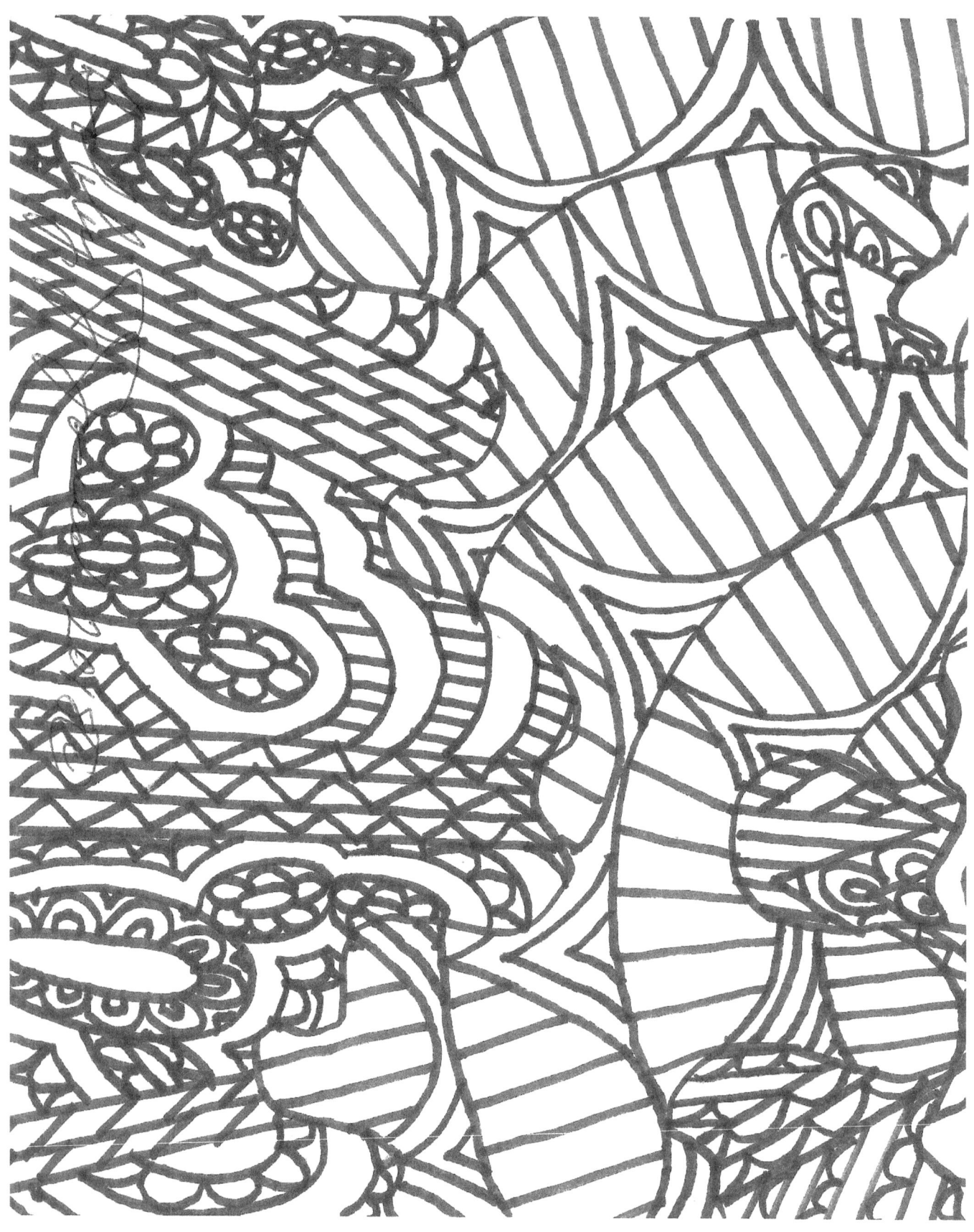

New Mexico Dreamscapes V

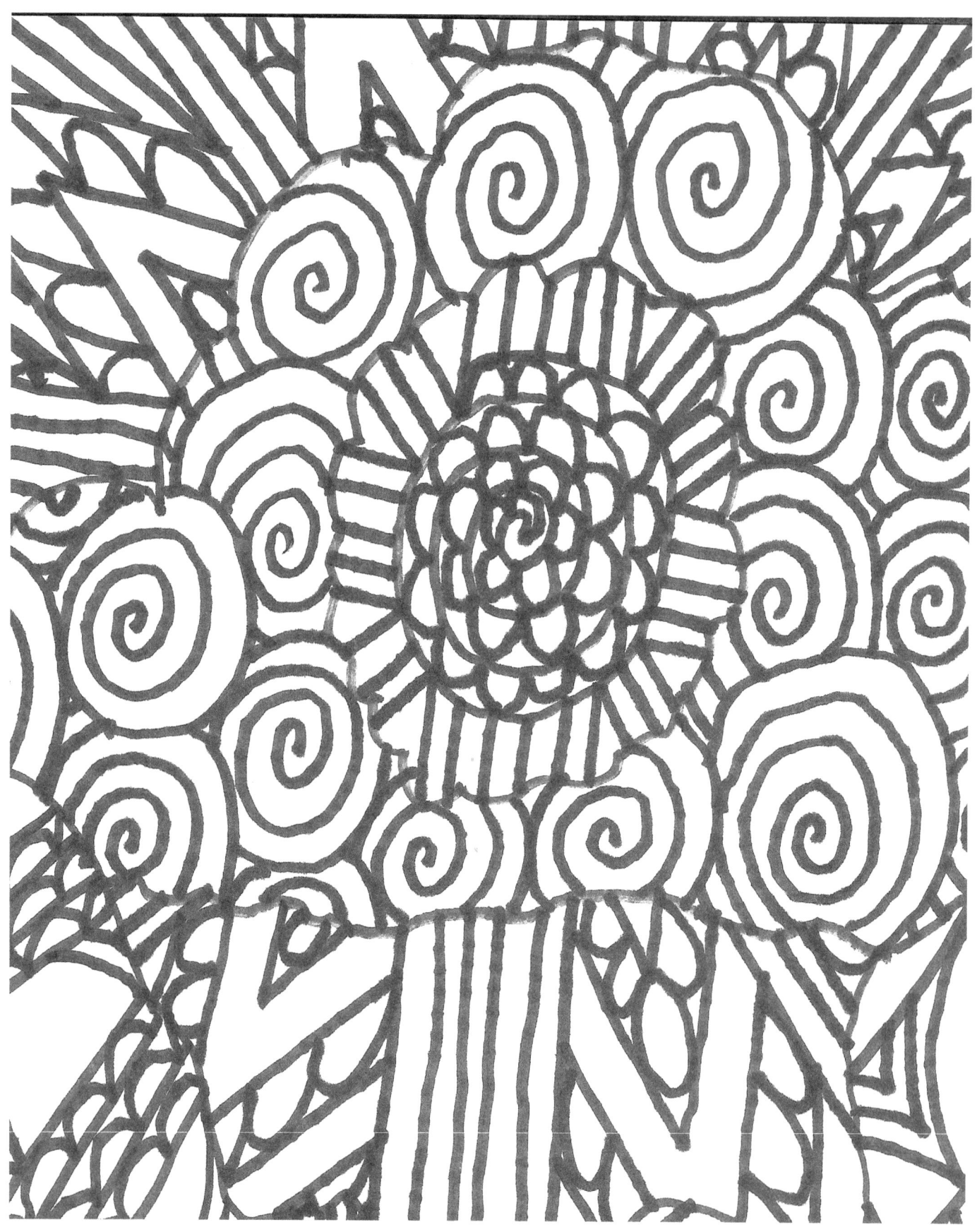

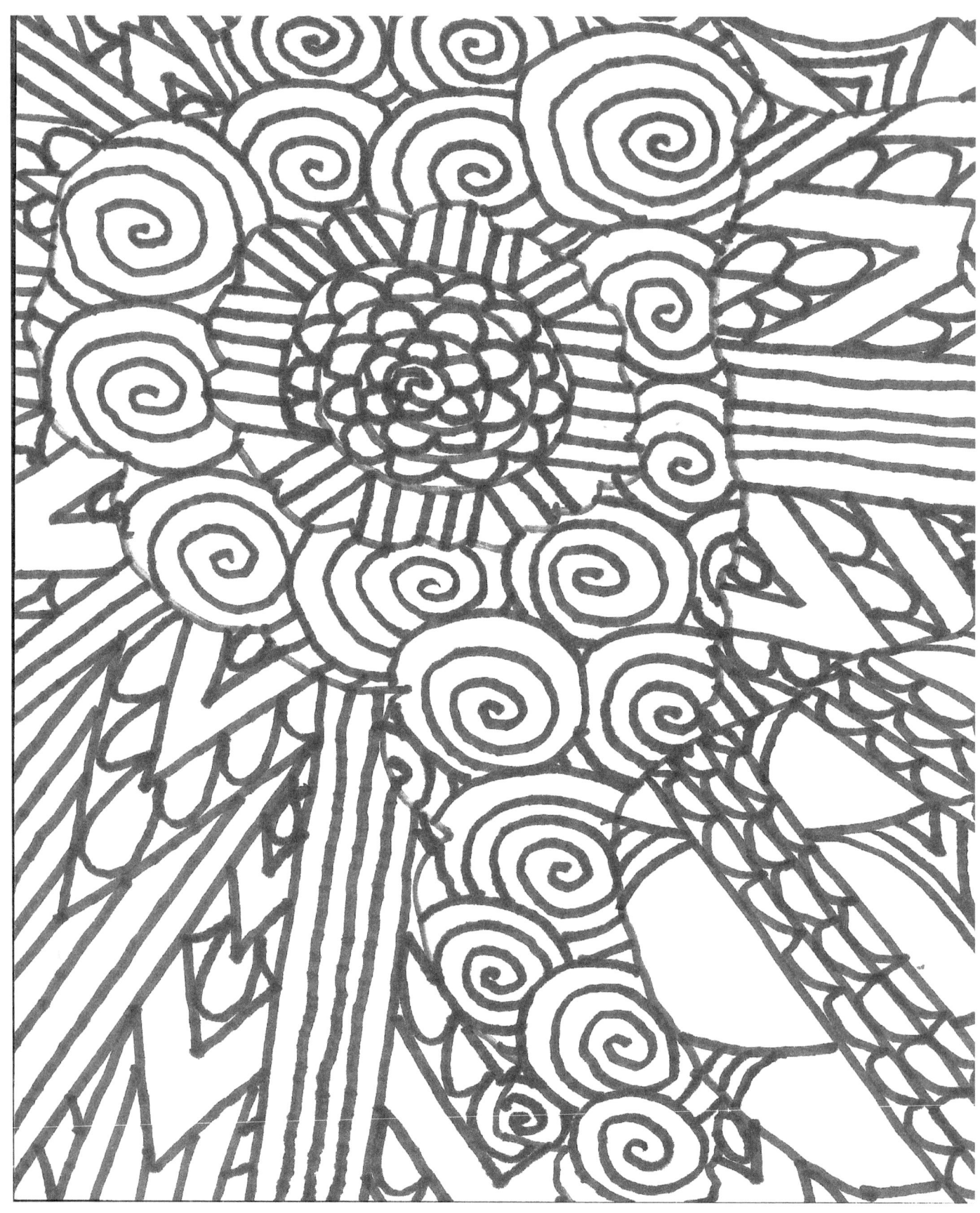

New Mexico Dreamscapes V

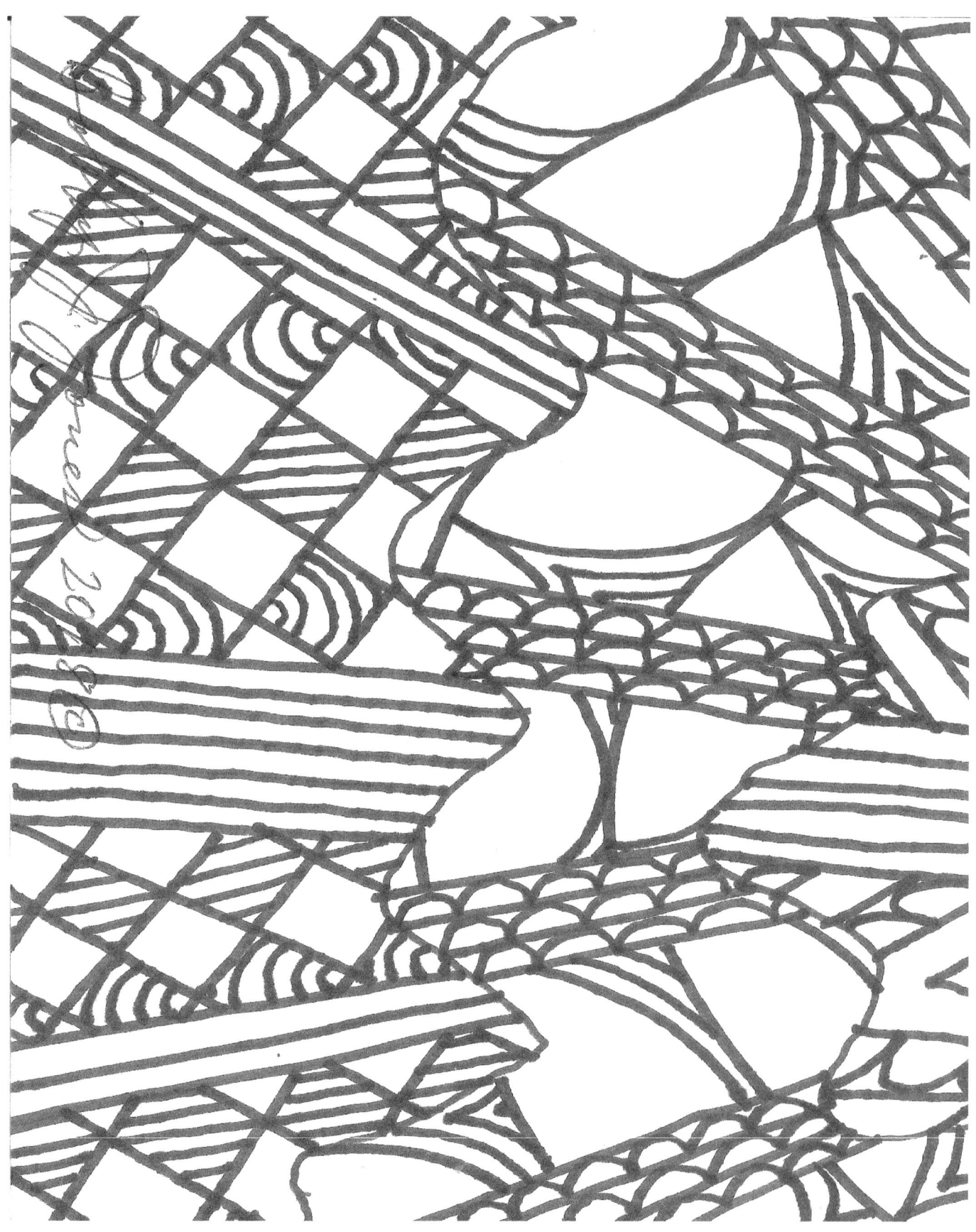

New Mexico Dreamscapes V

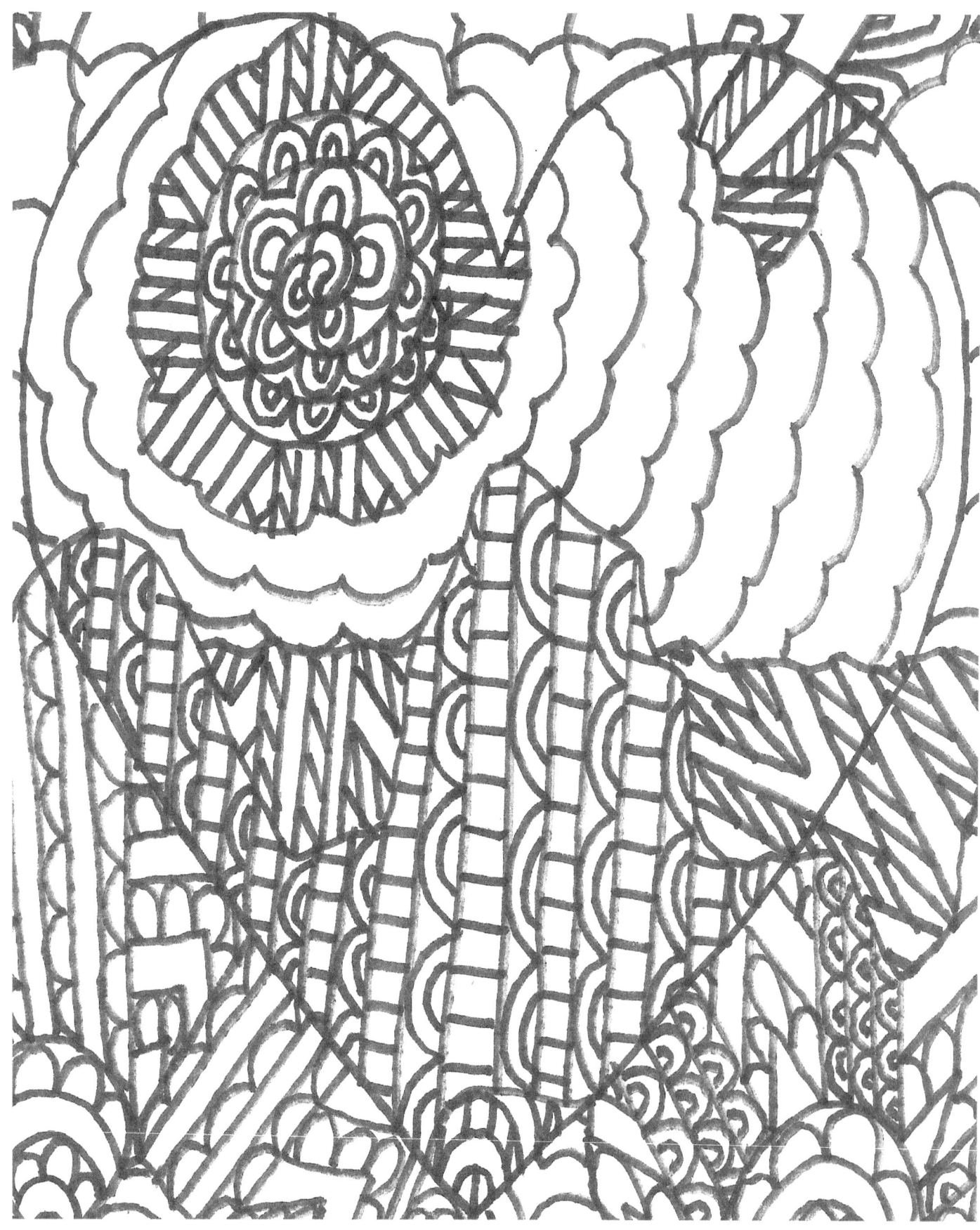

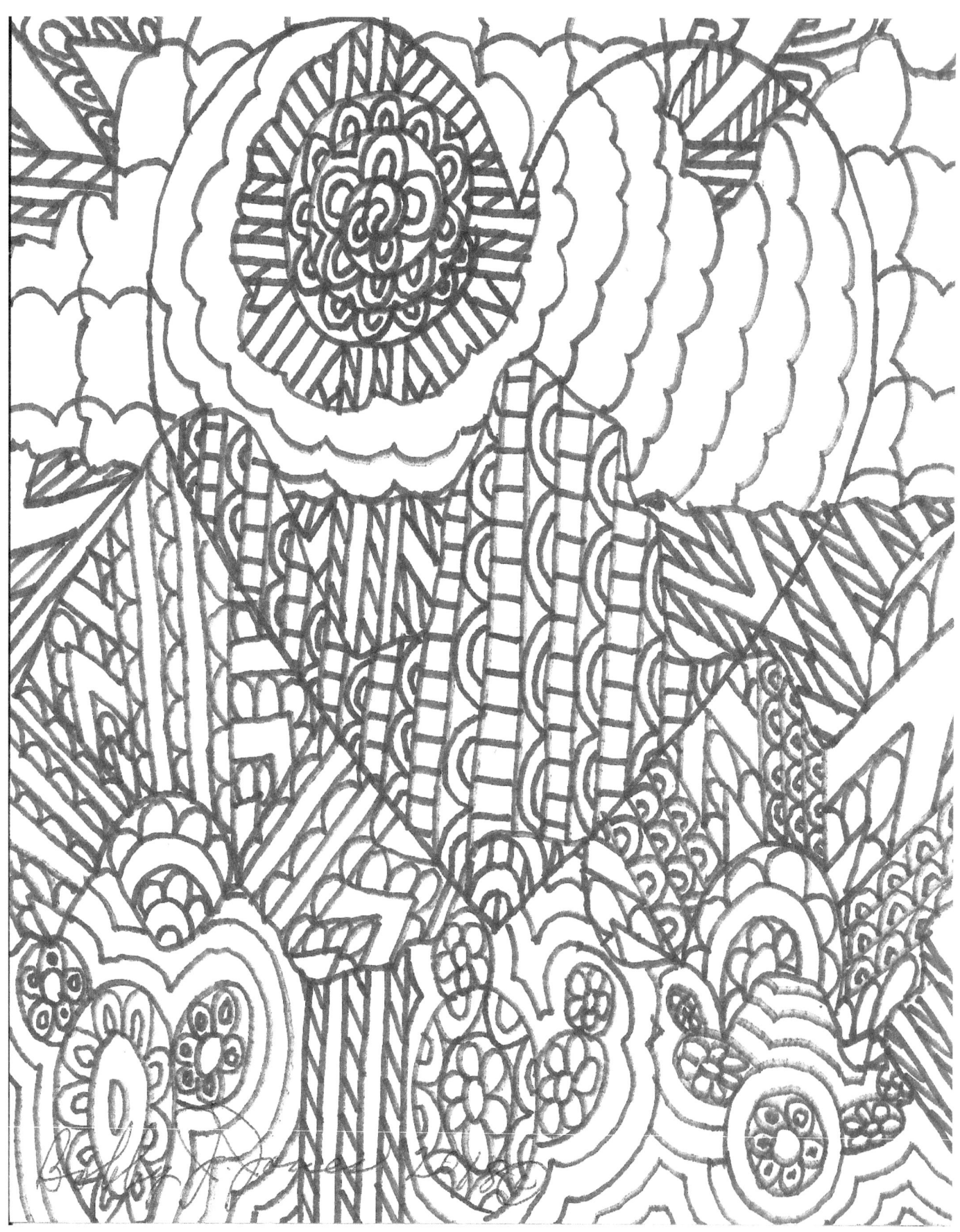

New Mexico Dreamscapes V

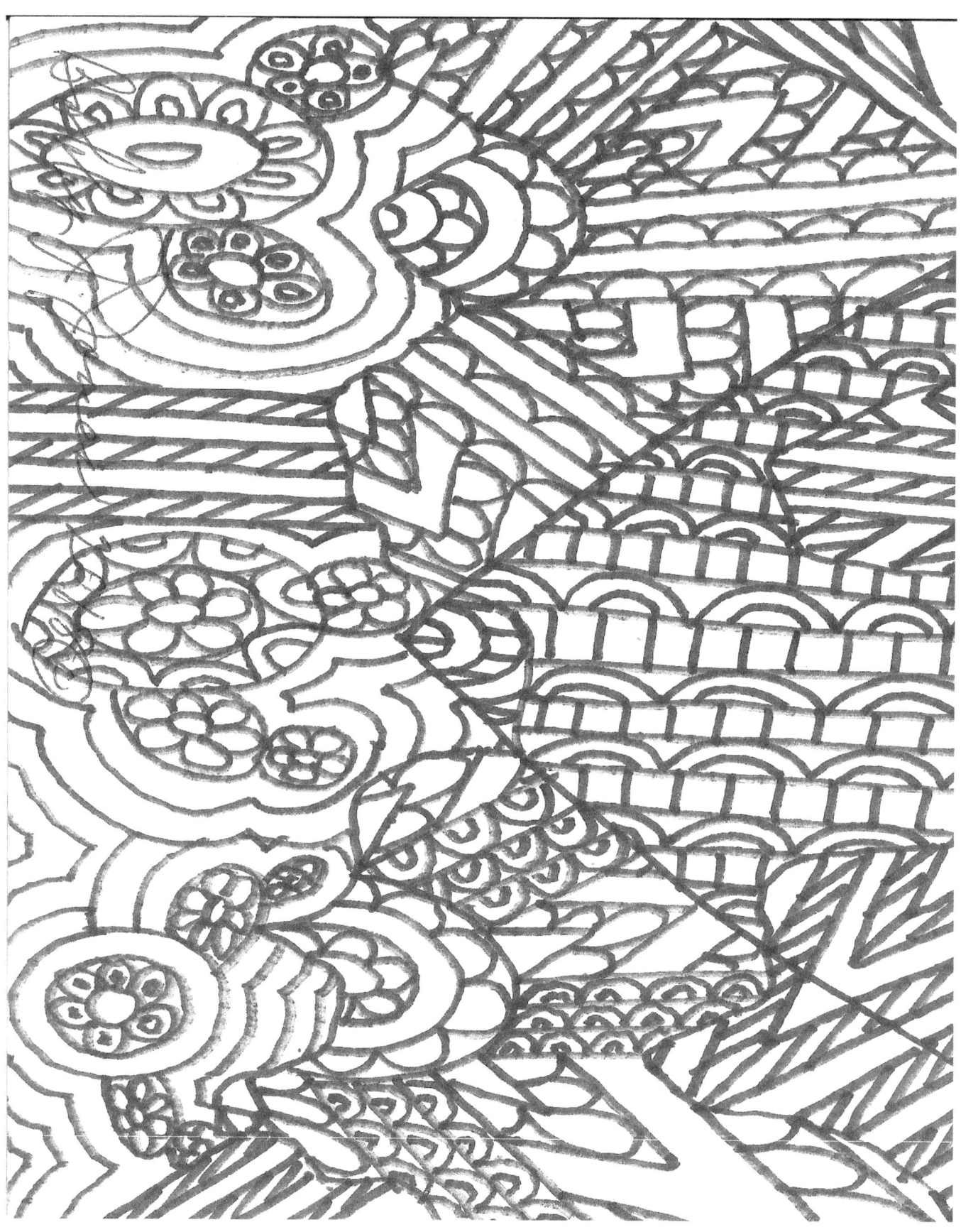

New Mexico Dreamscapes V

ABOUT THE AUTHOR

Bobby Jones was born at Reese Air Force Base in Lubbock, Texas in 1966. His family moved to Fort Worth, Texas in 1968. While growing up in Fort Worth, Texas, Jones attended school in The Fort Worth Independent School District. He graduated from Southwest High School in 1985 with honors.

Jones' father Toney Jones worked for General Dynamics as an Industrial Engineer for 25 years while Bobby's mother Kate Jones taught preschool for 20 years at Wedgwood Methodist Church, which became Genesis United Methodist Church in Fort Worth. Jones is the youngest son out of two daughters and two sons. He has two nieces, two nephews, and two great- grandnephews.

Jones attended Texas Tech University in Lubbock, Texas from 1985-1989. He received a BFA in Studio Art (Painting and Drawing) with honors in 1989. Bobby was a member of Alpha Phi Omega at Texas Tech and a member of Golden Key. Then he attended The University of New Mexico in Albuquerque, NM. He obtained a Masters of Art in Art Education (Museum Education, Ceramics, and Photography) in 1994.

Bobby moved to Southern California in 1997 and worked in retail management from 1999 to 2009 for various retail companies in the Palm Springs area. Jones returned to New Mexico in 2009. He worked in the customer service profession from 2010 to 2014.

Jones attended Central New Mexico Community College. Bobby obtained an Alternative Teaching Degree in Special Education and was inducted into Phi Theta Kappa. He started working for Albuquerque Public Schools as a substitute teacher and an educational assistant in Special Education.

He is currently a Preschool Teacher for Head Start with Youth Development Incorporated. He is also a member of First Unitarian Church in Albuquerque.

Jones is also an artist and creates two dimensional mixed media art that consists of his painting and drawing skills. His artistic inspiration focuses upon the environment of New Mexico. He has exhibited his work at The Factory on 5th, The Tortuga Gallery, The 606 Gallery, and First Unitarian Church's Social Hall.

He is currently preparing for an art exhibit at The South Broadway Cultural Center in January and June, 2019. His art entry for The 28th ArtsThrive Exhibit was accepted by the art jury members. Three art pieces will be on display at The Albuquerque Museum starting October 19, 2018 in New Mexico. Jones will be featured in one of the collective art exhibits at The Tortuga Gallery in 2019 in Albuquerque, New Mexico.

His artwork appeared in The Desert Sun newspaper (Palm Springs, CA) in the special edition of the first year anniversary of 9/11 and the 40th anniversary of The Kennedy Assassination. Jones also created an art gallery on Facebook, Bobbo66Art Gallery. He invites everyone to look at his art creations.

The artist freehands these original images in this coloring book. Jones does not use computer software programs, rulers or t-squares to create these beautiful images. He enjoys seeing the imperfections in his work. The imperfections are what make Jones' work uniquely original. Jones suggests to the people that buy this book. They can doodle on the blank pages opposite the blackline images or create their own dreamscapes. He is creating a series of coloring books and is creating images for his next coloring book for children of all ages.

New Mexico Dreamscapes V